PRODIGAL
Daughter

A
JOURNEY
WITH
MARY

by Patricia A. Santy, MD, OP

New Hope Publications

For additional copies of this book, contact:

New Hope Publications
PO Box 10
New Hope, KY 40052
270-325-3061
www.newhope-ky.org
Ask for stock #3460

ISBN: 978-1892875-85-3

Cover art: *The Rosary* by Camille Engel. Used with permission.
www.camille-engel.com

Dedication

To my daughter, Alexandra Richert,
and my brothers,
Paul and Skip Santy
and
to Annie, Carol, Dori and Sophia, my sisters

The first gulp from the glass of natural sciences
will make you an atheist,
but at the bottom of the glass,
God is waiting for you.
—Werner Heisenberg, Father of Quantum Physics

Table of Contents

INTRODUCTION

Many thousands of books have been written about Mary, the Mother of God, including theological treatises, essays, and prayers. There is even a theological area of specialty known as "Mariology" that studies Mary's role in the Bible and tradition. Most of these books are Catholic in origin, because it is primarily Catholics who firmly believe that Mary enjoys a unique and special role in Salvation History. This role is not conceived as separate from that of Jesus, our Redeemer, but in concert with His role. And, it is a role that has become increasingly important since the Death and Resurrection of her Son and the birth of the Church. Mary spent thirty years with Jesus; the rest of the world claimed Him for only three. Since her Son has reconciled us to the Father, she has come to be seen as the embodiment of the Church, the Bride of Christ, and the role model for what each human can become.

So, why is there so much controversy about Mary and even angry disagreements between Catholics and many Protestant denominations? At the foundation of these disagreements is the belief that somehow reverence and honor given to Mary detract from and diminish the worship that ought to be given to Jesus Christ alone. I have had many a painful discussion with my fellow non-Catholic Christians who denounce me and angrily claim that I will be going straight to Hell because of my sincere love for the Blessed Virgin.

"She's just a woman who happened to give birth to the Messiah." "She's nothing special that we need to spend time thinking about her." "She is virtually non-existent in the New Testament—she plays only a very small role and seemingly none at all during Jesus' ministry." "Jesus Himself dismisses her in several key places in the Gospels, and that clearly shows how unimportant her role is."

These attitudes give me great pain when I hear them and I often wonder if such attitudes give Jesus pain also. I think about how sons and daughters (especially sons, I suspect) come to the defense of their mothers when someone says something negative or downright insulting about them (from "your mother wears Army boots" to "you're a son-of-a-bitch"). Isn't it quite a natural response to fight? To make them take back their insult and apologize?

I know that is my response. Many times in private revelations from saints that are approved as "worthy of belief," we have learned that both Jesus and Mary have asked the faithful to make reparation for the many blasphemies and insults directed against them. I would imagine that Jesus, the Son of God and also the Son of Mary, might be particularly desirous of reparation for the insults, ingratitude and outright blasphemies directed against His beloved Mother.

Of course, few Protestants believe in the apparitions of Mary that we Catholics hold dear to our hearts such as Guadalupe, Lourdes or Fatima. They see those apparitions as demonic and a tool of the devil to lead us to Hell. How much more insulting could this attitude possibly be? And, how terrible that there are people who actually believe such a thing and how sad for them! All of us ask persons we know to pray for us and intercede for us with their prayers. How much more efficacious to ask the greatest saint in history, who also happens to be the Mother of God, to intercede for us with her Son?

Many writers have addressed these issues over and over again in various Catholic books and forums and it is not my goal to address them in this book. But I should point out that, contrary to what non-Catholics frequently say, Catholics do not *worship* Mary, but revere her and ask for her intercession in the courts of Heaven. This is very natural, since we see her as the greatest of all saints and we believe she enjoys a special place among all the saints and angels in heaven, and, as Queen-Mother, a special intercessory role with regard to her Son, the King.

Maximilian Kolbe, the great martyr and saint from World War II and the founder of the *Militia Immaculata,* wrote, "Never be afraid of loving Mary too much. You can never love her more than Jesus did."

So, this book is not meant to argue with my Protestant brethren or to be a Marian apologetic. My only hope is that all my readers might grow to love and appreciate Mary half as much as I have, since I owe her a great debt. The Father loves me and welcomed me home; the Son redeemed me; and Mary led me unerringly to her Son.

While many books have been written about Mary, this is the only book (and will likely continue to be the only book) written about me and my personal journey back to Jesus and faith in God. I don't carry around any strong sense that my life has been particularly special or spectacular in any way, but I have been blessed and I felt called to write my story—a story of an ordinary sinner who slowly and surely was guided by Mary back to her Son and to the One, Holy, Catholic and Apostolic Church. The lessons I learned from all my mistakes and sins are not original to me, and there are many people like me out there who have been blinded to Truth by any number of psychological traumas they have suffered and endured in their lives. These are the kinds of traumas that haunt you throughout your life, destroying the possibility of real love or peace. My story is one of a serial sinner who was in denial about God and Truth, and who but for the grace of God and the intercession of Mary, would never have found either. I detail in the first chapter the dream that was the impetus for me to write this book, so I won't go into it here. The poems that open each chapter have stories of their own, however, and I should explain them.

About the time I started writing the book, my daughter and I undertook the herculean task of cleaning out my garage at home. I found a box of a dozen or so old notebooks from my high school and college years (which I used to call my "Think Books"), when I considered myself something of a writer and poet. The notebooks contained all my old poems in handwritten form, as well as various writing ideas and snippets. I admit that I composed a lot of (bad) poetry, but even so, I had a few poems published in fairly reputable magazines back then.

I thought it would be fun to go through those notebooks and re-read the poems I had written some fifty years earlier, most of which I vaguely remembered as being about teenage angst and doomed love and things like that. Much to my surprise, I discovered that almost all my essential conflicts and concerns over the course of my life were contained in these early poems—so much so, that I decided to begin each chapter of the story of my circuitous wanderings away from and then back to God with one of them. I make no claim as to their quality; I only claim their accurate recording of my thoughts, feelings, and hopes from my youth. Each poem has its own story, and amazingly fits neatly into a portion of my journey. In a way, my life has been a bit like the Big Bang in that my youth had all this great potential, and at some point it all exploded out into my life, drifting away from its origin, like an expanding universe. Now, at this point of my life, all the pieces of a cosmic puzzle have been fully exposed and are coming back together in a great contraction and recoalescence. Just as cosmologists suggest that the universe will expand to a point and then slowly start to contract, so my life is moving inexorably back to THE origin of all things: God.

Patricia A. Santy

CHAPTER 1

THE MYTH OF MYSELF

Reminiscences of the Future

*Today
The sun will rise and pass among the clouds;
Sequences do not deviate from the patterns
My mind creates each day.
My life will be as it has been.
Except,
I will meet a man
Who shatters patterns
And sets the world in different frames.
The sun will rise and pass among the clouds,
But I will be released.*

The Beginning of the End

The best place to begin is usually at the beginning, but in the case of my story it actually is more reasonable to begin at the end; otherwise everything that has happened to me in my life might appear rather random, when in fact, it makes perfect sense as a puzzle fully assembled makes sense, but only because the pieces are now in their proper order and you can now see the whole picture. Future proves past.

So I will start this book at the beginning of the end. The end of the end is still in the future and in God's hands, but everything in between has either happened or is still happening. I don't want you to get the idea that everything important has already transpired in my life—it hasn't. I hope for a good long time to worship and praise in this world before I pass on to the next, but, of course, you never know.

Why call it "the beginning of the end"? For me, this phase of my life, in which I had already called a truce with old age and settled into the trenches, was abruptly interrupted by something quite extraordinary and unexpected. For fifty years I had prided myself on being an atheist. But I always told myself I was an atheist with an open mind. *Truth* with a capital T was my passion, and I can't think of a time when I didn't tell myself that finding Truth was the most honorable and important thing that one could do in life, especially as a scientist and a doctor, which I was. And, it is fitting that Truth was my salvation as well as my downfall. For truth (little t) can be manipulated and ultimately deceive, but Truth (capital T) cannot be anything but itself.

When it came to belief in the Almighty, as a young child I had unquestioningly accepted that He existed (as young children generally do) up until the Great Disillusionment which came at the age of twelve. After that, I just as unquestioningly believed that He didn't exist. I spent years accumulating evidence that shored up this belief. And yet…. for some reason which I couldn't quite put my finger on, I never felt completely satisfied with the evidence. This "scientific" and professional skepticism ran parallel to the unpalatable reality that something was also missing from my personal life, though the two realities didn't converge in my mind until much later.

I dutifully read Dawkins and Hitchens, Harris and Dennett—the four horseman of the new atheism. As a psychiatrist, I was especially intrigued by Dennett and his explanation of consciousness and the idea that free will was compatible with naturalism. I had explored modernism and naturalism and taken in the resulting atheistic world view from the perspectives of the evolutionary scientist, a political journalist, and neuroscientist, as well as from the perspective of ethics, morality and psychology.

But reading the thoughts of these clever minds was unsatisfying and only made me restless to find more compelling arguments. The evidence, the proofs, the arguments presented just didn't *feel* right. Not so much because I was into feelings or that I valued feelings over reason, but precisely because the logic of their position on the matter was not in sync with the vehemence or intensity with which they presented those arguments. I thought that most of the arguments were tainted with emotionalism, rather than reason. It mattered too much to them that God didn't exist. It was like He COULDN'T exist—or else everything in their world view might be invalidated.

If God truly didn't exist, then why was it so important to prove that He didn't exist? You can't prove a negative, after all.

Instead of confirming my own rationale for atheism and sole belief in the material world we perceive with our senses, I was exquisitely aware that the arguers' affect did not correlate with their reason. In psychological terms, their presentations and books always had that whiff of what we refer to as "cognitive dissonance"—or, that mental willingness to hold contradictory positions or positions that, when reduced to their essence, seemed to be untenable. What I wanted was a rational explanation of my own cognitive dissonance!

I stopped thinking about the whole issue for quite a while as my career took off in my 20s and 30s. Who had time to think about God when they were actually living their lives? But the dilemma festered in my mind all the same. Then, in my late fifties, when despite being near the end of what would seem to be a very successful career, it seemed to me that life had not worked out quite the way I had wanted, and in spite of my professional success, I reluctantly admitted to myself that I was unhappy. After 27 years of marriage I was getting a divorce, and although the divorce was entirely my own initiative, brought about by the delusion that if I changed everything in my life, I would find the secret to happiness and finally find my "soulmate," I felt that I was a victim. I wallowed in my victimhood and outrage at the universe. I had been cheated, I believed. Hadn't I done all the proper things and made the right choices that everyone said would lead to happiness? My career always came first. Hadn't I always fought against those sexist stereotypes that led to so much inequality between the sexes? Hadn't I been told I could have it ALL?

Things only got worse as I frantically I tried to dig myself out of the hole I found myself in—financially, psychologically and spiritually. I was no longer sure what to believe in anymore, but books and scholarship had never failed me, so I turned once again to the intellectual defense. I decided to reinvestigate the unresolved God issue that I had abandoned some years before. Unsure where to begin, I read someplace that next to Einstein, one of the greatest human minds that ever existed—possibly the greatest—was Thomas Aquinas. I had never read anything by him, so I resolved that I would look into his writings. Little did I appreciate at the time what that resolution involved! But I did start to read the *Summa*—and lo and behold! I found in St. Thomas a kindred spirit, albeit one that was light years more intelligent than I! His five arguments for the existence of God were straightforward and non-emotional. This led me to read other books and arguments. Something long dormant began to quicken in my mind and heart.

But let me go back a little bit to give some context to what came next.

Ten years prior to my divorce, I had had the opportunity to travel to Portugal to participate in a research symposium sponsored by NATO that related to my work in psychiatric aspects of space flight. As part of the trip, our NATO hosts hired a bus and driver for six or seven of us which took us around the entire country for a week of sightseeing prior to the meeting. It was a wonderful adventure in the company of some of my favorite military colleagues in psychiatry and psychology. As part of the experience, our driver took us to the shrine of Fatima. I can remember as a child being fascinated by stories of the Blessed Virgin's apparitions at Fatima in Portugal to three young children.

Shrine of Our Lady of Fatima in Portugal.

The stories were linked in my mind to the rosary, because it was at about the same age that I had heard the stories that I had started praying the rosary. I realized that I felt rather sentimental about this particular Catholic devotion (or so I told myself at the time) and while visiting the shrine, I was able to purchase a rosary that had been blessed by the then-current Pontiff, John Paul II, from a vendor. I told myself that it was just a "meditation" technique that I was going to try when I got home (talk about cognitive dissonance!). But John Paul II was an intriguing and rather charismatic figure for me. I remembered reading about his attempted assassination by a Kremlin stooge some years before. John Paul believed that the reason he did not die from the assassin's bullet was because the Blessed Mother deflected its course away from his vital organs. As a result, the Pope had revisited the secrets of Fatima and gone to the shrine in Portugal himself. His papal motto was *Totus Tuus* ("totally yours"), which indicated his consecration to Jesus through Mary. I was unexpectedly moved by the story that the Pope had some years later visited his assailant in prison, and had forgiven him! As a student of psychology, this seemed counterintuitive to normal human nature. Despite my interest, when I returned from the trip, I packed the souvenir Rosary away and forgot about it.

I found the rosary from Fatima in a box from the garage I was going through in preparation for moving to California shortly after my divorce was finalized. I was stressed out and anxious about the move, which was a big deal for me and involved a lot of bridge-burning and many unknowns. My ex refused to speak with me; my daughter was eager to move to California where she hoped to go to college; and I just wanted to get out of the state because in addition to not speaking to me, my ex was already involved in another relationship. Needless to say, I was not, and it pained me just to think about spending the rest of my life alone. My brother and his wife issued a lovely invitation to me to move to Fresno, California where they lived and to "grow old with them." They even had a house into which I could move if I was able to take over the mortgage payments. I decided to pull up roots and start over in a place where I knew no one except my brother and his wife. The discovery of the Fatima rosary coincided with my increasing stress levels, as well as my newfound determination to examine my commitment to atheism as I tried to put back together the shattered pieces of my life.

I renewed my intention to once and for all end my doubts about God one way or the other after I moved to California. At first it wasn't the foremost thing on my mind, but increasingly as the months rolled by, I became more and more obsessed with finding out the Truth. Did He exist or didn't He? I read books pro and con. I pondered their meaning and their evidence for one perspective over another. I found that every piece of evidence on the "pro" side always brought me to the edge of a precipice beyond which I could not go without falling into an unknown abyss. I could not see the other side of that abyss, but its bottomless darkness was utterly terrifying, and it was always at this point that I would turn back and seek out more evidence. No matter which path I followed in my quest, I always seemed to reach the same precipice, and the fear it filled me with made it too overwhelming for me to make the final leap, hoping there was solid ground on the other side.

I grew frustrated and the whole situation reminded me of the scene in *Indiana Jones: The Last Crusade* where Indy had to step out into nothingness to make the final "leap of faith" to find the Holy Grail in order to save his father's life. "You must believe, boy," his dying father whispered in the movie. But I was not brave as Indiana was, I'm afraid. I would stare down from that precipice into the infinite darkness below and simply could not make myself take another step. I couldn't deal with the reality that logic and reason could only take me so far and no further and that to get to the other side of the gorge, I had to *have faith*. I wondered why this was such a stumbling block for me. Had I been so hurt by the past that I was never going to trust again? I thought about all the "leaps of faith" we take in science. I believe that atoms and molecules and protons and electrons exist, but I've never seen one—or any—of those smaller particles. I believe that Love exists, but you can't scientifically describe or measure that reality either. I would think, "I WANT to believe in You, God, but I was hurt before and I can't let myself be hurt like that again." So I would once again turn around, go back to the books, and search for another path that might lead me to the other side *without* belief.

But the many perspectives on faith that I was reading, especially some that came from hardened atheists who set out to debunk God and who were converted in the process, were all having an effect. Although I harbored grave doubts about and grandiose detachment from the Almighty, I became very aware of an almost desperate desire on my part to want God to be real.

This was because it was becoming clear to me that only if He is real do the concepts of *Justice* or *Truth* have any meaning. How can we assess Truth, for example, without an objective standard of Truth? All you get without such a standard is your own personal truth (with a little *t*), and to my mind that is illogical. Further, only if God is real does the *meaning of life* take on a dimension that is worthy of the human mind. Nihilism, so prevalent in my generation, was abhorrent to me, and it seemed that nihilism was the ultimate consequence of "little *t*" truth.

Finally, I came to realize that the search for God is nothing more and nothing less than a search for and understanding of one's own self. Although we humans are not God, we are presumably made in His Image, and so there must be some correlation. On the other hand, He would have to be so far beyond us that we could never fully understand His ways. He is perfect, we are flawed—not by design, but by our own choosing. But we are blessed with the gift of free will, and further blessed with the gift of Time, so that, unlike the angels, we are able to change our minds and return to the Lord if we trespass against Him. A further gift—and it can be a gift—is doubt, which by its very nature allows us to question not only the existence of God, but also our own movement away from Him. Only when we are in darkness can we fully begin to appreciate the light. I am certainly not the first person in history to wrestle with the idea of God or Faith, and many people, much smarter than I could ever be, have written extensively on this very topic.

But I am the only one who has written on the topic as it pertains to me and my particular struggle with big and little truth/Truth; and it is in this struggle that God was allowing me to look through the window of my own humanity to find Him.

As I said previously, when I was a child I was very religious with a childlike, unquestioning belief in the goodness of God; later, I scorned the very idea of God, and I have been at practically every point in between those two extremes at one time or another.

The search for God, the struggle with faith, is a search for meaning, a search for understanding one's place in the universe, a way to bring order out of chaos and separate light from darkness.

Ultimately, the only purpose served when the very human need to connect with the Infinite is mocked and ridiculed, is the *dehumanization* of mankind—a process that eliminates the spark of the Divine that exists within us all and which separates us and elevates us compared to all other animals on the earth.

All of these thoughts went through my mind during this time. I also drew from my professional experience as a psychiatrist, journeying deeply into the pain and despair of a human soul. Sometimes the journey made me fear for my own sanity and that I might lose what makes me who I am. But I have always been aware, in the distance, of a light that marks the path back to my own self, and have always managed to find my way back. I cannot decide if that luminous signpost is simply a part of me...or if it is the God I was finding increasing comfort in believing in.

When I was in high school and college, I was very prolific as a poet—though not necessarily very good. Nevertheless, revisiting my old poetry gave me an insight about myself that I was unaware of at the time. I could see that even then, I was searching for God, in spite of all my declarations rejecting Him.

My Last Crusade

The waffling back and forth went on for more than two years. The preponderance of the evidence surprisingly seemed to suggest that there was a God out there, but I was stubborn and could not allow myself to accept it. I started wondering why all the paths from all the different books led me to the same precipice, but never took me across to the other side. This in itself was a valuable clue about the nature of reality. Did taking that final step across the precipice to the other side require something that was "not dreamt of in our philosophies"? Was that what this whole thing was about, I wondered? Did I just have to believe in my heart, but not in my mind? I had for some time been regularly reciting (I would not call it *praying*) the John Paul II-blessed rosary, not just for meditation and stress relief, but out of a quiet desperation at night and in the dark. I felt terrible desolation. All the painful abandonments and betrayals in my life would take over my mind and I would feel unwanted, unappreciated, unloved. I was filled with a horrible emptiness and what I thought must be the ultimate sense of loneliness: by myself in a vast empty reality. I began to wonder whether life was worth living. I tried to pull myself together by going on a regimen of diet and exercise to try and help me focus (isn't that what all the self-help books suggest?).

In the early mornings, I would often go for a walk on the paths in my little community. On the morning of April 16th, 2012, the pathway was particularly peaceful and shady, and a walker could listen to and observe nature all along the two-mile route that I took. I often used the walk as a time to ponder my unhappiness and frequently talked to myself as I was doing on that particular day. "Tomorrow, I'll try reading that new book. Maybe after that I'll re-read Aquinas and go over the Five Proofs again and then…"

Suddenly my thoughts were interrupted by a voice that was not my own. The Voice was not a whisper, but was clear and insistent, warm though perhaps a little exasperated. I have tried over and over to reconstruct in my mind the sound of that Voice but I cannot adequately describe it at all. Only two words were spoken, but the implication of those words—the mere existence of those words—quite simply knocked the breath out of me and brought me to my knees on the dirt path in an explosion of awe and amazement. And then, suddenly, suddenly, everything was different, and the pieces of my world shifted and set themselves into a new and spectacular realignment. The next thing I knew, I was on the other side of the precipice.

WHEN, DAUGHTER?

Two Dreams

A week or so after hearing the Voice (which I knew in my heart was God), I had a very vivid dream that stayed in my mind and was so unusual that I wrote it down. I often had intense dreams, but their meaning and relationship to events in my life was always fairly straightforward such that understanding them was simple. But in this new reality in which I found myself, I was already discovering that everything—even the smallest most uninteresting development—had meaning; nothing was unimportant, and everything was connected. As a psychiatrist I tended to minimize dreams that patients brought to me, since I thought there had been an overemphasis on them by Freudians. Yes, of course they said something, but that something was usually not very profound—or so it seemed to me. Yet this dream stuck with me. I wondered at the imagery (usually my dreams were very boring or just plain scary); the colors were magnificent (usually I dreamed in black and white). I didn't understand the ending (what exactly were "the 144,000"?). I tucked it away into my mind until I had further information.

April 30, 2012: The Knight

She looked up at the stunningly beautiful cathedral in the bustling and noisy cityscape. It sparkled like a precious gem, lying in the middle of a refuse pile. The arches and spires reached upward, while the statues of angels and various saints anchored it to the dying city. She felt a sense of awe, but at the same time felt comforted, as if she were entering a secret place, safe and well-guarded from the tumultuous and dirty affairs of the world. Walking slowly up the marble stairs to the entrance, she pondered what she would say to the priest in the confessional when it was her turn to go in.

To her surprise there was no one inside, either in the lovely wooden pews or even in line for the sacrament of reconciliation in the old-fashioned confessional in the rear of the nave. Surely this was the right time? The stained-glass windows cast a shimmering glow over the interior of the church, giving it a rather unearthly aura so very different from the gritty and unwholesome atmosphere of the city outside. Except for the colorful shafts of light from the windows, the interior was unlit.

She made her way to the ornate stall of the confessional where one of the doors on either side was open and a small green light was on, indicating that a priest was inside and waiting for penitents. She went in. The little sliding door through which one talked to the priest in confidence did not open, and she remained kneeling and strained to see if she could hear the person on the other side talking to the priest. After a while, she realized there was no priest and no other person there.

The Knight.

Time passed. The sense of being alone in the small reconcili-ation room and the overall emptiness of the church began to make her uneasy. Some part of her remembered that this was only a dream and in dreams everything always felt strange and made sense at the same time. For that reason, she did not get up and leave to find a priest (which would have been the logical thing to do), but instead, she curled up on the small floor and fell asleep.

Sometime later, she awoke refreshed, yawned, arose and opened the door. The nave and narthex were still completely devoid of peo-ple and the flowers before the altar were now withered and dry. The stained glass glow had dimmed from bright colors to a subdued palate of grays and dark shadows, and she understood that signifi-cant time must have passed. Carefully she made her way back to the cathedral entrance, opened the large wooden doors, and went out-side. What she saw stopped her in her tracks. The city in all its grimy and debauched glory was completely gone; and in its place was a vast, seemingly endless desert scape without a sign of life or vegeta-tion of any kind for as far as her shocked eyes could see. It seemed to her that some giant hand had simply picked up the church, plucked it out of the world and dropped it into this alien landscape. She gazed out at the small hills and valleys of sand before her and wondered what it all might mean. Shielding her eyes from the brightness of a setting sun, she looked around to the west and then to the east. Just at the reach of her vision, she could see a small dark object. Focus-ing on it, she was able to eventually make out a figure of some kind, black against the horizon, growing larger. The figure seemed to be moving in a rhythmic fashion toward her.

As it became more distinct, she realized it was a man—or rather, a knight in full armor—galloping toward her on a white stallion in full medieval battle array. Her first reaction was to be annoyed. Was this some cliché remnant of the past when women were weak and oppressed by the male hierarchy? Was she to be rescued by a "knight in shining armor?" All that emancipation for nothing? But the thought evaporated, and with it her annoyance, as a sense of expectation gripped her. She was fully in the dream again and every-thing in a dream made sense.

The knight, who looked more and more impressive the closer he came, finally reached the spot where she was standing and expertly pulled his horse to a halt. The knight looked down at her for a moment, then reached out toward her, his metal glove upturned in a non-threatening manner. She could see his beautiful eyes, visible through the visor of a helmet, which was decorated with two long feathers projecting from the top, one white and one red. The eyes blazed with both kindness and ferocity. She noticed that at his side there hung a sword with a jeweled hilt and some symbols near the top of the blade that she could not make out.

"Who are you?" she asked in a loud voice, though she might as well have whispered since the silence was so profound that even his approach on a galloping horse had made no sound.

"I am one of the 144,000," he replied. "Come with me."

Without hesitation she trustingly gave him her hand, and he effortlessly lifted her up into the saddle behind him and they rode off.

The next dream took place more recently and is the reason I am writing this book. I don't know or understand fully what use this autobiographical screed may have, but I feel compelled to write my story, and specifically to highlight the role that Mary, the Mother of God has played in it. But more of that later.

February 24, 2019: The Illuminated Manuscript

She had just finished reading the hour of Scripture she set aside each Sunday as a goal for the year. The last word of Deuteronomy was completed and she closed the Bible, feeling very drowsy and warm since it was chilly and she had turned on the fireplace. In her mind, she calculated that she could get away with taking a short nap before she finished her weekend chores. She closed her eyes, drifting off at once.

In her field of vision, completely taking it up was an ancient-looking, illuminated, medieval manuscript. It looked like pictures she had seen of such manuscripts and there was a drawing at the upper left hand corner at the beginning. The handwriting was too small to read and the picture was indistinct. She could not make out the words.

She said, "I can't read it."

An illuminated manuscript.

Immediately the manuscript became magnified. The picture was now clear and she could see it was Our Lady of Fatima, with her white veil trimmed with gold and a crown upon her head. Despite the enlargement, the words remained unintelligible.

"I can't read the words, Lord."

Again the manuscript enlarged, as if under a magnifying microscope; but the words were fuzzy and did not become any clearer.

Frustrated, she asked, "Why can't I read it?"

"Because you will write it."

The Myth of Myself

So, if the meaning of these dreams isn't crystal clear to you, then you are in good company, because it wasn't very clear to me either. I mentioned a puzzle earlier: you know how when you are putting together one of those 1000-piece puzzles that take forever to finish, you start by finding one small area where the pieces obviously fit together and just work on that section? It's only later as all those different sections come together that the image of the puzzle as a whole begins to make some sense. This book is going to be a lot like that, I'm afraid, so I ask that you bear with me for a while.

When I started to write this, the puzzle of my life was slowly assembling itself in my own mind. While searching online for some inspiration, I came across the *Litany of Humility*. I saw the Litany on a website I was browsing and it immediately held my attention, because if there is one virtue I definitely lack, it is humility. This troubled and troubles me greatly still. I remain captive to my pride and vanity, despite all my good intentions; and when push comes to shove, these bad habits continue to put distance between me and God.

Since coming back to the Catholic faith six years ago after hearing God's Voice, I wanted very much to be a saint, or—barring that possibility—at least increase my holiness; and seeing the Litany, it struck me forcibly how very often my PRIDE was a direct obstacle to any chance of increased sanctity. I even sometimes worried, for good reason, that the very desire to be a saint—a GREAT saint like Thomas Aquinas or Catherine of Siena—was in itself an expression of that pride: the need to excel and be first in everything, to be praised and honored and extolled. This particular need, to be perfectly honest, had been a constant motivating force for most of my life and this made me sad. It was always about ME ME ME, I thought with regret.

I could take little comfort in the thought that I was a true product of my culture and my generation: the narcissistic generation. You see, I came of age in the 60s, the decade when malignant narcissism, dormant in Western civilization for centuries, first began to manifest itself in all its destructive glory. Human nature had not changed much over time, but human philosophy had taken a turn toward the unreal and subjective a few centuries before. My generation was the unfortunate product of this philosophical monster, which had been nibbling away on the human spirit surreptitiously for a long time.

Lucky generation! At least we all thought so at the time, basking in and celebrating this disastrous new freedom, this orgy of self-indulgence. I and my fellow "freedom fighters" in the women's movement had access to the newly-developed birth control pill (halleluiah, baby!) which happily made the consequences of sex irrelevant, thus completely freeing us (especially women) to revel in random acts of fornication. Women were liberated! We burned our bras (I never actually burned mine, but I did stop wearing it for a few years). We were inundated with information and smarmy platitudes of female power and seduced by the liberated sexuality of the women's movement and *Playboy* into thinking and believing that women's equality and future were at stake. Jubilantly, we manned (an oxymoron, of course) the picket lines to demand equality for women with men and an end to the "oppression" of women as mothers and wives. "A woman without a man is like a fish without a bicycle," proclaimed one of my favorite mantras; and I remember thinking at the time how clever that silly meme was.

It didn't take many years for this movement to devolve further—for a devolution it was—into demanding social justice (another oxymoron) and then into a particularly pernicious psychological illness aptly named "toxic femininity." This latter iteration of the women's movement unabashedly sought the destruction of men and the family and gleefully celebrated the ritualistic murder of their own children.

Oh, how naïve I was! I freely bought into this myth of myself: there was nothing I could not do or be! No one—no man, certainly—could hold me back from anything. I didn't need men, or the institutions of dead white males. I was omnipotent and powerful on my own. I didn't need God or religion—outdated concepts from the primitive past when myth and superstition reigned. I was WOMAN, hear me ROAR!

Ha! So I abandoned the knowledge and wisdom of all the generations of mankind and then promptly succumbed to a completely new and improved set of self-serving myths and superstitions. How enlightened and liberated!

This new enlightenment told me I was no longer limited by my biology, no longer tied to history or tradition, no longer a slave to a male-dominated culture. I was especially no longer tied to God—and most importantly, no longer constricted by a reality in which God existed. I was encouraged to make my own history and to transcend my biology. Truth was whatever I wanted it to be. Of course you understand how seductive and mesmerizing all that was? Especially for me growing up in a very dysfunctional family. And, as I came to realize much later, almost all families are dysfunctional.

It is possible that I am overemphasizing the point, but this malignant movement of women's "liberation" fit right in with the transformation that began within me in my adolescence. The seed was planted that God, religion, and Christianity were not only ineffective but actually harmful to people, in that these beliefs gave them false hope and false values and ultimately betrayed them.

My parents divorced when I was 12 years old. It was not an amicable divorce, and the actual process of the divorce took place over several years at a time in our development when I and my two younger brothers were most vulnerable. Suffice it to say that at this stage of putting together the puzzle, an early exposure to Catholic schools led me to believe that God would immediately hearken to my pleas to keep my family together, and so I prayed quite a bit for several years, never doubting that my prayers would be answered.

My prayer was answered, it turns out, but not in the way I imagined. God had a different plan or, as I thought then, was clearly otherwise occupied and my little prayers didn't count for anything. Well, who needed Him anyway? The wretchedness I felt when the divorce and its consequences hit me was more than compensated by my anger at God and the universe in general.

That was the beginning of constructing an idol and believing in the myth of myself. Since I was all by myself, alone and on my own in the world with no one to help me, then anyone that I became or anything that I wanted to do was entirely up to me, myself and I, the new holy trinity. On the other hand, if I, or any woman failed, it must be because of the oppressive patriarchy.

What an unbelievably seductive perspective this was! Even now, decades later, I can remember the surge of power that thrilled me back then of taking my life into my own hands. Looking back, there was obviously a good side to it all in that it was this sense of power that enabled me not to become a victim of my circumstances which, as you, dear reader, will see, deteriorated into sordidness and abuse that led me to leave home and set out on my own at a very young age. Little did I realize that victimhood was the goal and highest achievement of my circumstances, but that would not become apparent until some years later in the evolution of the myth of myself.

Now I realize that the strength I exhibited then (some might even say courage) was really *grace*, an answer to my desperate prayers, though I never saw it at the time. It was grace that covered my extreme vulnerability and preserved me psychologically intact, though spiritually dry since I rejected God wholeheartedly and fully by the time I was a teenager.

I reinvented myself as an atheist and wore my new religion as a shield. I was going to be a scientist and a doctor, I decided, and so, I left behind all ties to fuzzy thinking about non-scientific things like religion and God, devoting myself to the future of me and to cultivating the myth of myself. The 60s and 70s were fertile ground for that exercise.

It was the second dream transcribed above, which I had prior to my 70th birthday that prompted me to write this book; and I knew that I had to be completely honest and truthful and not let my pride interfere in the process. Because, though in the eyes of the world, my life had been a success, I'm sorry to say it was a myth told by an atheist, full of pain, regret and sadness, signifying nothing—and then, by some miracle, it all made sense and signified everything.

But hopefully you will see that truth yourself in the pages that follow and as the connected pieces of the puzzle come together into the full picture.

Full of Grace

I did not come to fully appreciate the role that Mary played in my life until very late in the game. Again, as a child, I had a devotion to her, especially praying the rosary. I understood on some deeper level that she was also *my* mother, a mother who would never tire of my questions and confidences, never demean me or make me feel unwanted or unloved. Perhaps it was very natural that I focused all my rejected and unwanted love onto her and her Son then, just as I focused all the hurt and rejection onto them later. Recapturing that sense now in the present, I understand more fully how she truly is my spiritual mother and that with her tender love and guidance, I can make my own life right with God again. The deeper theology is fascinating and I hungered for it, but the bottom line was truly no different than when I was a child. The child was in many ways, much wiser than the adult. Or, perhaps, just much truer to self than the older, more bitter and cynical mythical version of the self I had become.

Consider Mary for a moment: an individual human woman, absolutely unique in all of human history. She is the daughter of God the Father, the Mother of God the Son, and the spouse of God the Holy Spirit. How incredible and special is that? She is the personified representation of Israel, the Church, and all humankind. She is what all humans could become if they modeled their lives on her. "Do whatever he tells you," she says at Cana, the last words of hers recorded in Scripture. Could there be a more succinct summary of what is needed to have Eternal Life? As Christ is the New Adam, she is the New Eve. Her "Yes" to the angel changed the trajectory of human history and put it back on a course that was planned from before the beginning of time.

So, where does Mary, the Mother of God, come into my story? My early devotion to Jesus when I was a child was formed through a love of Mary, the mother who gave Him birth. Being a woman, I think it was quite natural for me to identify with Mary. She filled the role of mother and protector for a vulnerable child. So, already at an early age, I was consecrated to Jesus through Mary. I went to Catholic school for kindergarten and first grade and during that time I learned my prayers and became especially attached to the rosary, or, as it used to be known in the early centuries of Christianity, the *Psalter of Mary*. Under the strict observance of the nuns who taught us, every day prior to the beginning of lessons, we children traipsed across the street to the church and prayed the rosary prior to Mass.

I remember fondly how saying the decades of Hail Marys was always a quiet pleasure and gave me great peace as a child. I was very proud of my little plastic rosary and kept it with me all the time.

The rosary played a big role in my reversion to the Catholic faith, as you have seen, and I want to demonstrate how Mary and her rosary are fundamentally connected to the whole concept of being "born again." Let's reflect on the phrase "born again." There exists considerable controversy over translations of the actual term in the various translations of the Bible, but sweeping all that aside, the phrase entered into frequent usage with the Protestant evangelical movement and came to mean converting to a belief in Jesus as Lord and Savior. In John 3:3 we are told the story of Nicodemus, a member of the Sanhedrin who comes to see Jesus one night and has the following exchange:

> "Rabbi, we know that you are a teacher who has come from God, for no one can do these signs that you are doing unless God is with him."

> Jesus answered and said to him, "Amen, amen, I say to you, no one can see the kingdom of God without being born from above."

> Nicodemus said to him, "How can a person once grown old be born again? Surely he cannot reenter his mother's womb and be born again, can he?"

> Jesus answered, "Amen, amen, I say to you, no one can enter the kingdom of God without being born of water and Spirit. What is born of flesh is flesh and what is born of spirit is spirit. Do not be amazed that I told you, 'You must be born from above.' The wind blows where it wills, and you can hear the sound it makes, but you do not know where it comes from or where it goes; so it is with everyone who is born of the Spirit."

Nicodemus answered and said to him, "How can this happen?"

Jesus answered and said to him, "You are the teacher of Israel and you do not understand this?" (John 3:3-10)

It is generally agreed that this passage is the source of the concept, however much disagreement about translation or meaning.

One night I was contemplating a different paragraph from John (*John 19:25-27*), where Jesus on the Cross gives His Mother to the Beloved Disciple and vice versa. Catholics believe that in this passage, by giving His Mother to the Beloved Disciple and entrusting the Disciple to His Mother, Christ established Mary as the spiritual mother of every Christian as well as the Mother of the Church.

It was in the holy womb of Mary, the woman who was chosen among all the women in all of history to be the Mother of Jesus, that Jesus the Man was formed; and it is spiritually through her that we are formed into other Christs and spiritually "born again." So, I thought, Nicodemus was correct in a way! We must reenter our spiritual mother's womb, and through her we are conformed to the image of Christ and reborn. Baptism is the symbolic way that this happens. As we are baptized with water, we begin a new life as members of the Body of Christ. Another thought hit me: the image of Divine Mercy where streams of blood and water pour forth from the heart of Jesus. Wasn't this reflective of childbirth? A woman's water breaks and the birth process begins, ending with the blood of the placenta emerging at the end. "Oh Blood and Water, which gushed forth from the heart of Jesus as a fount of Mercy for us, I trust in You," we say in the Chaplet of Divine Mercy.

It seemed to me that it was all tied together with being "born again." With Mary as our spiritual mother, we are born into the family of God our Father. That is how we are "born from above"—born spiritually—and still remain flesh. From the moment of her own conception in her mother's womb, Mary was "full of grace" as the Angel told her. This reality made her free from Original Sin, and during the Annunciation she was "overshadowed" by the Holy Spirit, the Third Person of the Trinity. Thus, her womb was consecrated and holy enough for the God-Man to be born from it into our world. Through her, we can be made holy enough to become part of the Body of Christ, her Son.

To Jesus Through Mary, as many saints such as John Paul II have said. In my head I heard again the Voice That Cannot Be Described:

WHEN, DAUGHTER?

I felt very humbled.

Litany of Humility

O Jesus! Meek and humble of heart, **Hear me.**
From the desire of being esteemed, **deliver me, Jesus.**
From the desire of being loved...
From the desire of being extolled ...
From the desire of being honored ...
From the desire of being praised ...
From the desire of being preferred to others...
From the desire of being consulted ...
From the desire of being approved ...
From the fear of being humiliated ...
From the fear of being despised...
From the fear of suffering rebukes ...
From the fear of being calumniated ...
From the fear of being forgotten ...
From the fear of being ridiculed ...
From the fear of being wronged ...
From the fear of being suspected...
That others may be loved more than I...
Jesus, grant me the grace to desire it.

That others may be esteemed more than I...
Jesus, grant me the grace to desire it.

That, in the opinion of the world,
others may increase and I may decrease ...
Jesus, grant me the grace to desire it.

That others may be chosen and I set aside...
Jesus, grant me the grace to desire it.

That others may be praised and I unnoticed...
Jesus, grant me the grace to desire it.

That others may be preferred to me in everything...
Jesus, grant me the grace to desire it.

That others may become holier than I,
provided that I may become as holy as I should...
Jesus, grant me the grace to desire it.

Rafael Cardinal Merry del Val (1865-1930),
Secretary of State for Pope Saint Pius X

CHAPTER 2

THE GREAT DISILLUSIONMENT

Saints and Sinners (A Song)

When I grow up, I'll be a saint,
And make my mom and daddy faint;
I've always been so good before,
But one day I will say no more.

They always had high hopes for me,
But never asked what I desired.
I follow all the well-laid plans;
Do all the tasks that are required.

I'll soon become respectable,
And get engaged sometime, somewhere.
To make my mother happy,
To make my daddy care.

But then they never could explain
What happens when I've done all this?
What happens next? I ask them how
Could I ever live as they do now?

When I grow up I'll be a sinner
And be my own kind of winner;
Not for mother, not for dad—
Since I have dreams they never had.

Exile

With the end of the story out of the way, I can now go back to the beginning, to the start of my self-imposed exile from God, and try to understand what happened. As a piece of the puzzle that is me, this is central and the foundation from which all the other pieces radiate. I think of it as "the great disillusionment."

My parents, mismatched from the very start of their relationship, were never happy in their marriage, and I became aware of that truth when my own hormones and attraction to the opposite sex kicked into gear. Not that there weren't many clues even before then.

My mother was especially unhappy and she had a way of letting everyone around her know that she was unhappy and exactly what she was unhappy about. One particular incident stands out in my mind in which all her complaints about my father coalesced into a single symbolic event.

She had gone away for a week somewhere (I don't remember where) and during her absence, my father had built on his own a brick fireplace and patio outside our home. Pop was a whiz at building and fixing things, but his job was a garbage collector working for the local branch of the Mafia who had fingers in many businesses in New Jersey (his father, my grandfather, also worked for them). He picked up garbage and cleaned out the homes of people who passed away and had his own dump truck that my younger brother and I used to ride in sometimes with him. It always smelled of his pipe tobacco rather than of garbage, and it was always a bumpy, exciting ride (no seat belts in those days) sitting on the front seat next to him. He wanted to surprise Mom with the outdoor fireplace and so told her nothing of his plans before she went away.

The evening she returned, we picked her up at the bus station and the ride home was clearly already tense, even before we got back to the house. I was aware enough even at the age of nine to pick up on the tension, but had no idea what was behind it. My father, in his sometimes ingratiating manner, tried to bring her around.

"I've got a surprise for you at home," he said to her.

"I'm not in the mood for surprises," was her only response.

Nevertheless, as soon as we got home he pulled her around the garage to the back yard to show her his brickwork. I stood excitedly nearby waiting for her reaction, which I expected to be positive and pleased.

It was neither. In fact, she tore into my father both verbally and physically as if he had shown her evidence of his being a murderer and was implicating her in the crime. I remember she called him every bad name I had ever heard in my young years, and several that did not register at all with me.

The gist of it was: "Here we are on the verge of losing our home and not being able to buy food, but you (YOU!) go and waste time and money on a stupid project instead of actually finding a REAL job instead of that toady job collecting garbage. WHAT KIND OF A MAN ARE YOU? YOU ARE WORTHLESS." This was more than I could handle, and I started to cry and ran into the house.

I sobbed in my room for hours that night. My mother had been so angry! I was sure that our family was breaking up, but it took many more incidents like the one above before the actual end of the marriage.

Shortly after the fireplace incident, we moved lock, stock and barrel to California and settled in with my mother's sister and her family (which included my five cousins). What prompted the move was my father's sudden relapse into malaria which he had contracted in Cuba during the war. This time around, he developed cardiac complications and suffered a mild heart attack which led to the doctor ordering him to move to a more moderate climate. I have always suspected that there were also serious financial considerations that led to the decision to move.

In California, my father got a job as a janitor at the local Catholic church, and we were able to rent, then buy a small home nearby. This only furthered my mother's vendetta against him, since his being a lowly janitor was rather humiliating to her. She hated the house because it was "in a poor area" and rather rundown; and, determined to improve our family income, she secured a job as a secretary at the University of California in the dean's office.

Thus the denigration and verbal abuse of my poor father continued for several more years. Pop was certainly not a perfect provider and he had a propensity to laziness (except when it came to sports), but he did not deserve the constant harassment and remarks on his character that came from my mother. There were only two things that my father really cared about (my brothers and I were a distant third in his priorities): baseball and the Marine Corps.

He had grown up in a large Italian Catholic family and was the next to youngest of five brothers and one sister. He was remarkably gifted in sports and prior to WWII had played professional baseball in the farm leagues. His one big chance came as a relief pitcher in the Show for the Washington Senators. It lasted only briefly and the story that came out of it, and which my father told often, was how "Joltin' Joe" DiMaggio hit a home run off him and then after the game took pity on the young pitcher and told him he was signaling his pitches by the placement of his foot. This was one of my father's favorite stories, and along with tales of his adventures in the Marines during the war, it was always a hit with my brother and me.

My Dad's baseball career was interrupted by the War and rather than be drafted, he joined the Marines, where he was immediately placed on their baseball team, much to his delight. He served with distinction at the Battle of Iwo Jima, where he was (ironically) shot in the foot and spent the rest of the war stationed in Hawaii. His brothers had joined the Army, Navy and Coast Guard and came through their battles unscathed. After the war, he ended up managing and playing on a minor league team for the Senators in New Jersey, where I grew up. Two of his brothers also played on the team, and some of my earliest memories are of the sounds, smells and rhythm of baseball.

Somewhere along the way he met my mother, who hated baseball, but agreed to marry him anyway. I believe that if my father had stayed in baseball—even in the minors where the pay was terrible—he might have been a happy man. But my mother was a social climber who did not care for the simple life and did not really feel that being married to someone who played baseball was befitting her image of herself. She nagged him until he quit baseball and took the garbage job in New Jersey (which she also hated, but which brought in more money). Pop's parents lived on a sprawling farm, not too distant from our house where they managed a vineyard for the local Mafia.

My mother came from a very different background. Her parents, one might say, were working-class aristocrats (at least my grandmother acted like an aristocrat). Both had come over independently on the boat from Southern Italy (near Bari), my grandmother stowing away on the boat at age 16 and arriving in New York without a penny to her name. She started a sewing business that was very successful, and then met my grandfather, who had his own business as an iceman (refrigerators needed ice to keep things cool in those days). They married and had three children; the youngest, Paul, was in the military stationed in Korea when I was born. My aunt Pauline and her husband lived with them in a sprawling old house into which my parents also moved after they were married. Paul Ceglia was killed while stationed with the military in Japan during the Korean War when I was 2 years old, and hence my youngest brother, born shortly thereafter, was named after him. When my father got the job as the Mafia's garbage collector, we were able to move into our own home in a new neighborhood.

It was one big, unhappy chaotic Italian Catholic family with lots of shouting and fighting and gesturing in both English and Italian. This carried over into my own family, and the fighting and bitterness and resentment just piled up over the years. Things came to a head when my father's heart problems made it difficult for him to work, and we moved to California. Things between my parents then went further downhill when my mother got the job at the University of California in Riverside working as a secretary for my soon-to-be stepfather.

Medically barred from athletics, and working part time as a lowly janitor, my father became a "bum" in the words of my mother, and his natural inclination to laziness was enhanced tenfold.

It didn't take long for my mother to start an affair with her boss at the university, who was an elder in the Mormon Church and married with four children. It wasn't long before she told my father that she wanted a divorce, something unheard of in those days in a Catholic family, though neither of them was very deeply Catholic to begin with. I always suspected that my father's job as a janitor at the nearby Catholic church, St. Catherine's, was more of an act of mercy on their part, than anything else; but it was enough to keep the family going to Mass every Sunday. I was more involved in church matters because of my brief stint in the Catholic school when we lived back east. I walked the half-mile to St. Catherine's frequently after school to say the rosary. My prayers to save my family became increasingly desperate as the situation between my parents continued to escalate. I begged and pleaded with God to keep my family together. I wept and demanded that God do something to prevent the breakup. As the oldest, I felt the weight of responsibility for keeping the family together. My younger brothers were oblivious to what was going on—Paul was completely wrapped up in sports, and Skipper was only a baby.

My parents divorced just as I turned 12. My father moved out, and we suddenly moved into a much larger and newer home with Glen, who left his wife and four young children for my mother. For a while, my father tried to make the best of it and would sometimes pick up my brother and me and take us to the airport to watch the planes take off. He didn't have much to say that was positive about Glen or about my mother.

I was very angry and frustrated with God who had not only ignored my prayers, but seemed to be actively making things worse. I had trusted in Him, but instead of my prayers getting answered, I was now living in a nightmare world. The university dean was a pervert and had a cruel streak that soon manifested itself to my brother Paul and me. Skip was just a baby at the time, and it was only years later that he became the object of Glen's perversity. Our stepfather made sure that Paul and I knew we were "white trash" and worthless. He made fun of us constantly and my mother did nothing about it, or perhaps she never noticed. At night, he used to slip into my bedroom and sit on the edge of my bed and talk to me in a fatherly and condescending voice about how the best thing that had ever happened to me was him. This eventually led to touching me and playing with my body. I was terrified of him.

Meanwhile, my mother, always rather vain about her looks (she was beautiful, in fact) began to act strangely towards me. I wanted to take piano lessons. She was very talented in piano—a prodigy with perfect pitch—and decreed that I had no talent and she wasn't going to waste the money. I was allowed to date boys, but when they would arrive to pick me up, she would greet them at the door "dressed to kill," as they say, and the entire date would be spent on him talking about how incredible my mother was. To say I did not like this would be a gross understatement, and any potential the boy had in my eyes immediately dropped to none. It was the closest I ever came to actually hating my mother. Mom would constantly go on about my weight, my hair, my posture, the big, goofy glasses I had to wear—any and all physical aspects of me. I felt ugly and inferior. It didn't take long for me to act the part. The only area in which I could "best" her was in scholastic achievement. And I focused on that with a passion. It never occurred to me that I was living in a fairy tale and that my mother had morphed into a wicked queen or stepmother. I realize now that she must have sensed on some level what was going on between me and her new husband. Life became hell. Why was God continuing to punish me, I wondered? All the more reason to hate Him who had put me in this position in the first place.

My brother, who knew nothing of what was happening with me, decided to chuck all the prosperity we had living under my stepfather's roof and to throw in his lot with our father. He soon moved out of the house. It was almost a year after that when I left also and followed him to move in with my father. I hated my stepfather with a passion, and dreaded the possibility that I might blurt out to my mother at any moment what he was doing. What I dreaded more was the possibility that she would be enraged at *me,* not him. My resentment and anger toward God intensified. I never understood how my mother could not have been aware of what was going on, and in retrospect I realize how relieved she was when I finally moved out of the house.

It didn't take long for my brother and me to grasp that my father was not particularly interested in taking care of us. I was 16 years old and my brother was 15 when Pop decided to move in with a girlfriend who would support him. We were left to live in the dark, dank and sleazy motel by ourselves. With the help of some teachers at my school I was able to obtain a position working part-time in a chemistry lab at the university during the day in between classes, to get a job announcing baseball at the local park where my brother Paul played in the Colt League, and to write articles on baseball games for the newspaper. I had enough money for my brother and me to survive. I was soon made the manager of that one-night stand motel where we lived. This kind of thing happened to me a lot throughout the years. I suppose it was a testament to my capabilities and how

I was able to present myself. Wherever I went, I would eventually be placed in charge of things. It certainly wasn't because of anything conscious on my part, but probably reflected the high sense of responsibility that I projected.

But, something in me had changed for the worse when God had not answered my prayers. I was completely disillusioned with the entire concept of faith. What good is faith, I thought, if it can't even help you in situations like mine? The innocent, trusting and romantic young woman who had once actually considered becoming a nun faded, and in her place was born a tough, capable, but extremely angry and occasionally manipulative person. Instead of my grades plummeting like my brother's had, I was the darling of all my teachers in high school. They all believed that I was remarkable and competed in mentoring me. All were convinced I would make something significant of my life. I clung to their hope and covered up my own despair.

It was at this stage in my life that I made a conscious decision to become an atheist. At the same time, I became obsessed with the philosophy of Ayn Rand, who was herself an avowed atheist. As sure as I had been that God existed, I now believed there could not possibly be a God, at least not one who cared about humanity, and certainly not one who cared about me. I felt liberated and I began to excel in all areas of my life, which was now a testament to the phrase that I angrily repeated over and over again to myself: "I'll show them!" I took as my role models the Randian heroes and heroines, and it brought me great success.

Rand's philosophy was one of self-actualization combined with aggressive and personal selfishness as an ideal to strive for. I would imagine myself as a Dagny Taggart type heroine and repeat the pledge from *Atlas Shrugged:* "I swear by my life and my love of it I will never live for the sake of another man, nor ask another man to live for mine"—the oath the heroes swore on entering Galt's Gulch. It was a good attitude to one's life and there is much to recommend it, I still think, but it ignores something fundamentally human. And, of course, it goes without saying that a true believer in Rand would never live his or her life for God, either.

Thus, my self-imposed exile from my true home began.

I graduated from high school with honors and due to constrained financial circumstances I decided to attend the local university. I couldn't decide on a major, because I wanted to learn everything. In the end, I had multiple majors, but the two I loved most were biochemistry and literature. I was fairly determined to eventually become a medical doctor, and I truly enjoyed classes on physiology and biochemistry—but I also loved to write, and literature and poetry were equally important to me. I didn't want to give either of them up. My biochemistry professor, Dr. Norman, was a big influence in my thinking about this. He told me once that medicine was like studying the music from a beautiful grand piano, while in biochemistry, that piano is chopped up into tiny splinters of wood and you have to imagine how that lovely music was made. This metaphor excited me because I thought that what interested me the most was how these two diametrically opposite ways of viewing the world could come together. Was I interested in the music, or was I interested in what made up the individual notes? In the slivers of wood, or in the piano? What an intriguing puzzle!

Dr. Norman's imagery also gave me insight into why I loved literature and poetry. These were the expression of the "music" of mankind! This clash of world views within me has been a constant source of indecision and conflict all through my life. Both are valid in their own way, but I have come to appreciate that all too often, when too much emphasis is placed on the "splinters of wood," the beauty of the larger picture is obscured and even obliterated. I was always drawn to the image of the whole puzzle; but at the same time, I also enjoyed studying the pieces of the larger mystery. And, those pieces only had meaning because of the whole.

Does that sound pathetically abstract? My brothers are fond of telling me that I think too much, and they are entirely correct, because when you think too much, you also run the risk of missing the larger meaning of things. Yet, these are the things I used to think about, and still spend my time pondering today. I believe that my vacillation between these extremes, and my excessive pride in thinking that I would be the person who would finally integrate the dialectic, is what led to my vulnerability to the spirit of the anti-Mary, and to my exile from God.

The Spirit of the Anti-Mary

It has become rather obvious that something is wrong with Western culture. Many writers have speculated as to the root of a seeming decay in values and morality—in particular, with regard to issues of sexuality, gender and marriage.

This moral rot eating away at our nation and culture did not begin in my lifetime, but it is coming to fruition in it. What had been planted philosophically decades earlier was now certainly ripened. In a way, the entire culture was choosing to follow Eve's behavior, consuming the apple that only leads to banishment and the loss of paradise. I readily joined in the feast, consuming conventional morality and soon was nourished by the poisonous ideology of feminism. This toxicity is not accidental but is deliberate in two aspects: the human aspect and the spiritual aspect.

The human aspect of the poison is designed to cause women to despise their role in life as child-bearer, mother and wife. This necessitates the denigration of men, marriage, and family. It has led to hatred between the sexes, feminized men, and murdered babies.

The spiritual aspect is clear. Just as Eve's abandonment of God led to the doom of all her children and an abrupt separation from the source of all Goodness, so the feminist movement has led our culture into a denial of that Goodness, a denial of Truth, and a repudiation of Christ's sacrifice on the Cross.

Like many of my era, I was extremely vulnerable to the existing cultural trends of the 60s' sexual revolution, and I allowed something to take over my personality and attitudes toward those trends. There was, I realize in retrospect, a sense of nihilism and hopelessness that overtook my sense of life. I was desperate for love and attention—especially from men—but I was also desperate for attention from my mother. Not getting either need satisfied by my parents, I built up a seriously strong defensive wall around that need for a father's love, and I consigned to the nether regions of my mind the need for a mother. And that's when the spirit of the anti-Mary must have entered.

Carrie Gress has written that Satan's point of entry into many women is what she called "the Malcontent Heart" in her book, *The Anti-Mary Exposed.* Gress discusses in detail the cultural trends of the 20th century that made it easy for women like me to become vulnerable to such a toxic spirit:

> If there is, indeed, an anti-Marian spirit, what might it look like? Well, a woman in its grip would not value children. She would be bawdy, vulgar and angry. She would rage against the idea of anything resembling humble obedience or self-sacrifice for others. She would be petulant, shallow, catty, and overly sensuous. She would also be self-absorbed, manipulative, gossipy, anxious, and self-servingly ambitious. In short, she would be everything that Mary is not. She would bristle especially at the idea of being a virgin or a mother.
>
> Women have always desired equality and respect, but our current culture isn't seeking it through the grace of Mary; rather, the culture seeks this equality and respect through the vices of Machiavelli: rage, intimidation, tantrums, bullying, raw emotion, and absence of logic. It is this aggressive impulse—this toxic femininity—that finds pride in calling oneself "nasty," feels empowered by dressing as a vagina, belittles men, and sees the (tragically ironic) need to drop civility so that civility can somehow return again.[1]

When I was a child, I alternated between wanting to be a nun and thinking that there could be nothing more wonderful than having a big family when I grew up. I used to say that I wanted to have nine children (so that I could have my own family baseball team, I suspect). Suddenly in my teens I desired the dramatic opposite. In fact, I decided that having children would be at best a complete nuisance, and at worse, an impediment to my own self-actualization, and a damper on my dreams. I had decided to become a doctor, perversely because my mother suggested that I might want to become a nurse, a vocation which she had once aspired to. Also, it was my way of combining the feminist movement with my Randian orientation. Ayn Rand herself was no feminist, and specifically denounced the movement for it ideological inconsistencies. But ideological inconsistencies were the least of my emotional or intellectual problems.

As a consequence of my father's indifference and stepfather's exploitation, I became dependent on having men desire me; and because of my mother's abandonment and unwillingness to protect

---

1   Gress, Carrie. 2019. *The Anti-Mary Exposed: Rescuing the Culture from Toxic Femininity.* Tan Books, Charlotte, N.C.

me, I walled off completely the pain of not being loved and the fear of being unlovable, and focused on being smart.

I had been somewhat quiet and introverted as a young child in elementary school, and then in junior high and high school I found the "real" me: someone who was suddenly gregarious, opinionated and a little aggressive; overly interested in boys and dating; eager to shed any vestige of innocence or vulnerability and become one with the world, so to speak. I totally bought into the idea that women could "have it all" that was so popular then. I devoured Betty Friedan's book *The Feminine Mystique* and admired Gloria Steinem, subscribing to *Cosmopolitan*. I regularly perused *Playboy* magazine, to see what needed to be done to attract men and be considered beautiful and sexy. I spent hours obsessing about my looks. Of course, I also wanted to be the smartest person in the room at all times, like Dagny Taggart in *Atlas Shrugged,* and this was aided by the fact that I was very good in academic pursuits. I didn't hang out with the "mean girls" at my school—the cheerleaders and prom queens—but I was on the fringe of that circle and that was close enough. I became somewhat vulgar and risqué in my speech and equally comfortable hanging out with the guys who accepted me since I was also good in sports and thus commanded a certain respect. Underneath it all, though, I was an angry person. So angry, I had to work hard to camouflage it from everyone around me.

In short, I became the sort of woman that Gress described so accurately in her book.

No longer did I have any desire whatsoever for the religious life, and I was somewhat amused at some of my childish fantasies. Likewise, I no longer wanted to have children. What a nuisance they were for an independent, accomplished woman! Certainly women who wanted to become nuns or mothers were considered either deluded or fools, missing out on what life was really all about. Where once I went to church several times a week, Sunday was now set aside as a day for the worship of ME.

Once upon a time, I had considered Mary, the Mother of God, a perfect role model—the perfect daughter, spouse and mother:

> First, we know that Our Lady brings a unique spirit into the world as the Mother of God. She is the anti-Eve. Her yes reversed the

curse that Adam and Eve brought to humanity through Original Sin. Mary's fiat reverses Eve's rejection of God and his will for humanity. "As a woman brought humanity under the power of Satan," one theologian, echoing early Church Father St. Irenaeus, explained, "God would liberate humanity with the cooperation of a woman."[2]

Now, everything about Mary seemed so obviously weak, timid, vulnerable and dominated. That was not going to be who I was, I thought. I was going to be strong and take control of my life. I was not going to be a victim of circumstance. I was not going to let men like my stepfather ruin my life. I would show everybody! I wrote a poem-play about Adam and Eve and Satan, and I particularly remember a few lines of it: *"When gods have arisen in man who is free / the future is his who has the courage to be."*

Simultaneously bad poetry and bad philosophy.

No one in my family had ever graduated from college. I was determined to do so and then to go on to medical school. I was not going to let things like marriage and children interfere with these plans for my life. I was liberated and I could have as many men as I liked. Now that I had moved out of the home where I was abused and unwanted, I was invincible!

Such was the grandiosity of deluded youth.

Gress hones in on a remarkable piece of evidence for the source of the toxic femininity so prevalent today: it is the "embattled relationship almost all of these women (leaders of the feminist movement) had with their parents, especially their mothers. These founders of feminism, whom Chesler dubs the Lost Girls, were women from broken homes who carried around deep mother wounds inflicted by little to no emotional support and physical affection." Lesbianism was just a natural consequence of the maternal conflict especially: "It was a kind of desperate attempt to regain or obtain the love of their mother. Their thirst to fill this gap was displayed by their rampant homosexuality...."[3]

It was not a long span of time when this brand of homosexuality (and perhaps all homosexuality, since evidence now suggests that

---

2 Ibid, p. 10.

3 Ibid., pp. 68-9

all those "scientific" papers on the biologic underpinnings of same-sex attraction were likely incorrect) was entirely fashionable and teenage girls (and boys) were trying it out just as they would try on different outfits from a store to see if they liked them.

Despite all my transgressions, deliberate and otherwise, this is one trap I did not fall into. I cannot remember ever being attracted to another woman in a sexual manner, as much as I admired some. This lack in my experience and presumed cowardice in my behavior was pointed out many times to me while I still considered myself a feminist. I had other women coming on to me, but that didn't disturb me as I could always appropriately convey my lack of interest in such things.

Benedict XVI, when he was much younger, wrote a book called *Daughter Zion*, wherein he discussed the various Marian dogmas in the Catholic Church. In the book he clearly demonstrates how much emphasis God places on chastity for women by citing as examples the many barren women of the Old Testament, who compared to their fertile counterparts, were blessed by God. In this way, God actually "flips" the human narrative that emphasized fertility as the greatest accomplishment for women (and as a counterpart for men, the human narrative emphasized the importance of the older son who inherits, while frequently God chose the younger for special blessings). Examples of the infertile/fertile women were: Sara/Hagar, Rachel/Leah, Hannah/Pennina, and others. This emphasis on fertility for the sake of God and not man, culminated in the New Testament with Mary and the Virgin Birth. If you consider that sexual intercourse is actually a sacred act, that it follows God's command to "be fruitful and multiply" in Genesis, then this makes perfect sense. Having children is a blessed event, but was never meant to be a contest of who could produce the most male children for a dynasty—that is how humans see things, not how God sees them. All children are precious to the Lord. Sex was never meant to be an end in itself or purely for mindless pleasure as it is viewed in our own day. Of course it is pleasurable, but the pleasure is not the point. The point is creation. We are made in God's image, and God is the Creator. One way that human beings are the image of God is through the union of male and female that creates a living being from their own matter. Just as in the Creed we say that the Son is *consubstantial* with the Father; so is a human child *consubstantial* with mother and father. All creating that humans do (painting, writing, building, etc.) is a mere reflection of the fundamental act of creation inherent in the act of sexual reproduction. And that act is only a pale imitation of God's ultimate creative ability from which He creates form and life from nothingness.

God's blessing on the barren woman in the Old Testament and on the virgin (chosen barrenness) in the New, was His direct counter to pagan cultures' worship which often involved priestesses performing ritual fornication as part of idol worship.

Thus Mary becomes as the Virgin Mother of God, the epitome of both chastity and motherhood simultaneously. Nothing is impossible for God!

Bishop Fulton Sheen wrote, speaking of Mary at the foot of the Cross in the Gospel of John:

> At this moment on the cross we no longer have Jesus and Mary. We have the new Adam and the new Eve. Our Lord on the cross is the new Adam, the Blessed Mother at the foot of the cross is the new Eve. And we're going to have the consummation of a marriage, and out of the consummated marriage of the new Adam and the new Eve is going to begin the new Church of which John will be the symbol.

> And so the new Adam looking down now to the woman says: "Woman, your son." And to the son, he did not say "John" (he would have then been only the son of Zebedee) but "Son, your mother." Here is the begetting of a new life. The Blessed Mother becomes the symbol of the Church. And as Eve was the mother of the living, so Mary becomes the Mother of the new living in the order of grace.[4]

How blessed am I (and is everyone) to have Mary given to us as our mother so that we can choose to be born again through her. Like Jesus Himself, we are *spiritually* the children of a human mother and a Divine Father.

All of my childhood and early adult poems were written out of the pain and anger I experienced when I did not feel love from my

---

4   Dietrich, Henry, Ed. 1985. *Through the Year with Fulton Sheen: Inspirational Readings for Each Day of the Year.* Ignatius Press, San Francisco, p. 66.

mother or father in this world, and spiritually rejected the love from my spiritual mother and Divine Father.

I include these poems throughout this book at the beginning of each chapter to show the extent of that pain and alienation. At the same time, as I read them now with eyes that have been transformed by true love, I can see how even then in my life, at the start of my atheist rebellion, they were somehow predictive of my eventual return to the Catholic faith and to Him. My spiritual mother understood that pain even more than an earthly mother could. While I am only one of the many she has brought back to her Son and the Father, I venerate her with all my heart and thank her for her tender love and guidance.

The Garden Dream

She knew she was in a dream, but the colors and brightness of it all were so superior to her reality that she wanted to remain forever. She was in a beautiful garden of roses. Roses of every size, shape and color. The path she trod made its way from one incredibly beautiful rosebush to the next, each one a bouquet of fragrance and beauty. She had always loved roses and in many of the homes she lived in in her life, she had planted a special garden with special roses that she could retreat to.

As she walked along the path in the dream, she felt content and did not notice that the trail she took was oval in shape and that it was leading her back to the entrance to the garden. When she arrived back at the beginning, she discovered the path branched off at right angles toward the center. Curious, she decided to take it before making another round of the roses. There were interspersed rose bushes here also, she noted, along with lush grass and wildflowers all around. Up ahead she could vaguely see a structure of some sort and as she approached, she found herself looking at an incredibly beautiful and unique tree, laden with fruit, but not just one kind of fruit—many varieties of fruit! Every kind of fruit she could imagine hung from its branches. She stared at the tree, breathless. A woman's voice said, "This is the Tree of Knowledge. Do you know, daughter, where you are?"

She nodded. The voice asked again: "Do you know where you are?"

"I am in the garden," she replied.

"Not exactly. You are in THE GARDEN."

The girl could hear the capital letters in the voice. Suddenly she found herself being lifted up off the ground so she could have a bird's-eye view. THE GARDEN was spread below her and she could see it clearly now in its totality. Excitedly, she reached her hand into a pocket, and pulled out an old plastic childhood Rosary.

"I understand now," she whispered.

Once I was awake, the implications of the dream captivated me, and for some weeks I mulled it over and over in my mind.

In ancient Israel, the Temple was the dwelling place of God— God among His people—and it was considered the intersection between heaven and earth. Within the Temple was the Ark of the Covenant and on the Mercy Seat, between the two cherubim, was where God would come to be with His people.

The Temple also represented the connection between Israel and creation itself. Israel, the land of milk and honey, given by God to the people of God: Israel was the new Eden, established on earth as a precursor to the establishment of the true Kingdom of God. For the first time, I began to appreciate how important the rosary was and why Our Lady, the Ark of the New Covenant, in her many apparitions has urged the continual daily praying of the Rosary. Just as worship in the Temple was a return of mankind to Eden, so is the worship and contemplation inherent in praying the Rosary a return to that Garden Paradise, THE GARDEN.

Further, the Tree of Knowledge at the center of THE GARDEN is also the Cross of Christ. The path of roses leads unerringly to that Holy Tree no matter from which direction you approach.

The association of Mary with roses is evident even in the term *rosary,* which comes from the Latin word *rosarium,* meaning "rose garden." The rose as the queen of flowers has been a privileged symbol for Mary, Queen of Heaven and Earth, for many centuries. The rose also happens to be a symbol of Christ (think of the Christmas song from a poem by Goethe, *Lo, How a Rose E'er Blooming).*

This Marian symbolism is also present in Dante's *Paradiso.* His guide, Beatrice, invites him to contemplate among the heavenly inhabitants the beauty of Mary, the Mother of God: "Why are you so enamored of my face that you do not turn your gaze to the beautiful garden which blossoms under the radiance of Christ? There is the Rose in which the Divine Word became flesh; here are the lilies whose perfume guides you in the right ways."[5]

Dante also uses the rose as a symbol of the entire universe.[6] Incredibly beautiful examples of this symbolism are found in the Gothic cathedrals and their rose windows, the circular, stained glass windows that enhance the entrances of these churches.

Catholics believe that Mary is also the Ark of the New Covenant, as Revelation 11 and 12 testify:

> Then God's temple in heaven was opened, and the ark of his covenant could be seen in the temple. There were flashes of lightning, rumblings, and peals of thunder, an earthquake, and a violent hailstorm.

> A great sign appeared in the sky, a woman-clothed with the sun, with the moon under her feet, and on her head a crown of twelve stars. She was with child and wailed aloud in pain as she labored to give birth.

Mary carried within her womb the Word, the King/High Priest, and the Bread of Life. The Ark of the Temple had within it the Tablets of the Ten Commandments, the Rod of Aaron, and Manna which fed the Israelites in their desert wanderings for 40 years. Mary is intimately connected to the Temple and to THE GARDEN. As the Ark and *Theotokos*, she bears God, the source of all knowledge and life. She is also the New Eve, just as Christ is the New Adam. She is herself THE GARDEN, through whom God bestows on the world Christ and all that is good.

The rosary is a representation of THE GARDEN, or the Temple of Heaven in our present world, just as the Jerusalem Temple was in the ancient world. There is no longer a physical Temple in which to honor and offer our sacrifices to God. But we do this in the Holy Sacrifice of the Mass, and we do it also by praying the Rosary as we remember the mysteries associated with each decade. As we recite the Hail Mary we remember the *fiat* and the promise given to a young woman in Nazareth 2000 years ago. She carried in her womb

---

5   Dante. *Paradiso* 23, 71-75.

6   Ibid. 31, 1-3.

Jesus the New Covenant, and the seed of the New Garden of Eden. She herself is the Temple where God resides, her womb the Ark. Within her was planted the seed for all the fruit of the universe, her Son, fully God and fully man.

Many Catholic theologians have noted the transition from Revelation 11 to Revelation 12 and counted it as extremely significant. When it was written, the Bible did not have "chapters"— these were added to assist readers in later days. Thus, there is no separation except a paragraph between the two sections, the first of which describes the Ark in the Temple of Heaven, and the second of which describes "the woman clothed in the sun, with the moon under her feet."

I am no theologian, but I have always marveled at the description of the rosary as a powerful weapon against evil. And, after my dream I comprehended how powerful it was in the real battle of Good *vs.* Evil that consumes the world today. No wonder Mary is so insistent that we pray the rosary every day! We have in our midst not only the living God in the Eucharist but also THE GARDEN itself which can protect us against the evil of the world.

When Jesus told the Apostles that "the gates of Hell shall not prevail" against the Church He was establishing, He could not have given a more powerful weapon to keep out attacking demonic forces than the rosary of Our Lady.

Two important invasions of the Christian world were prevented by praying the rosary: the siege of Malta in 1565, and the battle of Lepanto in 1571. Both battles occurred when Islam attempted to conquer Christian lands, and both battles ended in the defeat of the overwhelming Muslim forces.

Malta was a strategically important island in the Mediterranean that was held by the Catholic Order of the Knights Hospitaller. When the Ottoman Empire tried to invade they had an overwhelming number of warriors compared to the knights. Yet, the Knights of God prevailed. Likewise, when a large fleet of Muslim ships met with Christendom's much smaller navy at Lepanto, they were repelled. The rosary played a key role in each of those battles, as I will relate later.

In my opinion, roses are the most beautiful of all flowers despite the thorns on their branches. These thorns exist to keep away anything and anyone who might try to defile their beauty. When you think of plants with thorns, the rose is likely the first to come to mind. There are many different types of roses, but almost all grow with thorns along their stems. Thorns are designed to protect them from predators that might otherwise decimate their flowers, fruit or foliage. The roses around THE GARDEN are designed to keep out the evil one. Make no mistake, Mary is a powerful defender of the Faith, and when necessary, this shield of defense also can become a sharp sword.

Further, Mary as the Ark of the New Covenant serves the same purpose as the Ark of the Old Covenant which was paraded before the troops in battle: her intercession is the most powerful weapon we have against the "powers and principalities" of the evil that rules this world. The Most Holy Rosary of the Blessed Virgin Mary is a key weapon in the battle against Satan and his minions.

Hymn to Our Lady of the Rosary

O Queen of the Holy Rosary!
O bless us as we pray,
And offer thee our roses
In garlands day by day;
While from our Father's garden
With loving hearts and bold,
We gather to thine honor
Buds white, and red, and gold.

O Queen of the Holy Rosary!
Each mystery blends with thine
The sacred life of Jesus
In every step divine.
Thy soul was his fair garden,
Thy virgin breast his throne,
Thy thoughts his faithful mirror
Reflecting him alone.[7]

---

7   From St. Dominic's Hymnbook, with the Order of Compline According to the Dominican Rite (1885). Burns and Oates, London. Hymn #146.

CHAPTER 3

A VICTIM OF BIOLOGY

To My Daughters Unborn

When I was young,
I thought of you and
What good girls you'd be.
I planned your schooldays carefully
Like all the loving mothers do;
And dressed the pretty birthday dolls,
Calling them by name:
Amalthea and Catherine.
You slept and cried and never grew,
Diapers wet, like real babies
Almost.

Then my mind was invaded by other loves
Other plans and this new world
Had no place for you.
Children together but I grew.
No time for you doll-child Amalthea
Not now maybe never.
Goodbye, my Catherine,
Child I never knew.
I was a doll mother once,
Almost.

Liberated (from Reality)

I continued to be a dedicated follower of Ayn Rand and her books in college. The "liberated" persona dominated every other aspect of me, and the myth of myself had fully taken hold. I dated a man who shared my interest in Rand and science fiction. He was someone I had known in high school. We made long-range plans for our careers and lives, but the subject of marriage or children never came up between us, since either might impede our quest for self-fulfillment and career advancement.

Jim was also a disaffected Catholic like me, and decidedly atheist. We were arrogant in our superiority and rejection of normal cultural values. We were not exactly hippies, since we believed that using drugs was detrimental to our brains; but I do remember once driving up to San Francisco so we could get a look at the then-famous Haight-Ashbury district where the "free sex and free drugs movement" had begun. We might have had moral objections to the drug aspect, but the "free sex" was fully embraced.

It was an eye-opening experience to witness the drug-addled, mindless behavior that went on in the sexual revolution's colorful capital. In some ways, the experience was absolutely repellant, but the sexual freedom (or should I say recklessness?) appealed to our late adolescent minds. While not fully embracing the movement's emphasis on "tuning in, turning on and dropping out," we definitely accepted its sexual mores.

Birth control pills were not so easy to get in the 60s, and we were oblivious to the realities of biology and never thought for a moment that unprotected sex could lead to anything but pleasure.

And then I became pregnant. I was only 17 years old.[8]

Jim was very supportive. He offered to marry me, I remember, and to this day I wonder how different things might have been if I had accepted. But I knew that his heart wasn't really in it. I declined and instead, we decided to make an appointment to see a psychologist/philosopher whom we admired. Nathanial Brandon had been the sidekick and lover of Ayn Rand, until she booted him from her inner circle and washed her hands of him. He was now practicing psychology in Los Angeles and we secured an appointment to discuss our situation.

---

8 I had begun college at 17.

He was also very supportive and referred us to a psychiatrist who, he assured us, would be able to help me to get an abortion. I was already almost 4 months pregnant and the situation felt urgent. The doctor (and his name I have totally forgotten as I blanked out most of the experience for many years afterward) was on the staff at USC-LA County Medical Center and within a few weeks, we had seen an obstetrician there who did abortions and was willing to admit me to have one. I lied about my circumstances, of course, because at that time getting an abortion was not an easy thing to do. I said I didn't know who the father was. I said I was suicidal and would kill myself if I had to have the baby (the psychiatrist recommended an abortion, and also recommended to me that I pretend to be suicidal, since that was one of the acceptable reasons to obtain a legal abortion back then. He knew I wasn't suicidal but documented in the chart that I was). I said that I had no support or help from my family (whom I never told, because, quite frankly, I wouldn't have had any support or help). I pretended to be pathetic and depressed (I wasn't really) and, of course, I added that a baby would totally destroy my life and my dreams to become a doctor.

The common thinking in the feminist movement at that time held that the "thing" growing inside a woman was a parasitic "clump of cells." They refused to refer to the baby as a baby. Things have not changed much to this day: women in pink vagina hats now ferociously proclaim that the baby inside is merely a "choice" and some even go further than that:

> In a segment yesterday [May 7, 2019] evening on Chris Cuomo's primetime show, a CNN contributor and former New York City Democratic politician made a particularly unscientific assertion in defense of abortion rights. During a discussion about state-level "heartbeat bills," which prohibit abortion after a fetal heartbeat can be detected, Christine Quinn claimed, "When a woman is pregnant, that is not a human being inside of her."

> Quinn, who served as the speaker of the New York City Council until 2013, is also a board member for the National Institute for Reproductive Health, a pro-abortion action fund. Her comment last night was, of course, factually and scientifically inaccurate by entirely objective standards.[9]

9 DeSanctis, A. CNN contributor: "When a woman is pregnant, that is not a child inside of her." The Corner at National Review Online. May 7, 2019.

I was admitted to the medical center, confident that I was doing the right thing for me. It was one of the worst experiences of my life. I had not realized that the nursing staff would be basically hostile to women seeking abortions. Unlike today, where killing your baby is celebrated in the most excessive terms, abortion at that time was not even legal in most states unless you had been cleared by a doctor. I was put in a large, dark room with about a dozen other women at various stages of abortion induction. The girl in the bed next to me was about my age, and she was in a great deal of pain. She had a tubal pregnancy and was slated for surgery. The girl on the other side of me was older and told me it was her third abortion and that it was "a piece of cake."

Since I was now almost five months pregnant because of all the hoops one had to jump through at the time, I was to undergo a saline induction type of abortion. The IV was set up—and then I was left alone. Completely alone. The beds on either side of me soon emptied and the nursing staff all but disappeared.

Someone from the billing office appeared at the bedside and started questioning me about my financial status and who was the father of the baby. I tried to be as pathetic and clueless as possible. The psychiatrist had warned me this would happen and coached me on how to deal with it. Eventually she went away. I felt proud of myself for being able to maintain the deception, but the pride quickly disappeared when the contractions began, induced by the saline.

Let me tell you about saline abortions. I didn't know it at the time, but saline enters the amniotic sac of the baby and it acts like a poison. The baby is being burned alive and kicks and jerks violently as the skin peels off. This painful process continues for 24-48 hours until the mother delivers a dead baby.

The cramping and pain were awful for me, but I was not being burned alive. I could distantly hear the whimpering of some women on the other side of the ward as they struggled with their pain. I suspected that I sounded very much like them. The nurses only rarely came in to check on us. Perhaps it was this, their lack of presence and their not coming to our calls, more than anything that made me think they were hostile to abortion. The hours passed and still no one came. The searing pains became more intense and closer together, and I wondered if I was going to die. At that point, I didn't much care one way or the other.

Not once during the entire ordeal did I ever think that I was killing another human being. I had swallowed the propaganda completely and been assured by all the experts that the clump of cells inside me was not yet human, and I firmly believed it. I didn't think about God or Mary or anything from my Catholic background; instead I focused entirely on all the benefits that this was going to bring to my life. When I met with Dr. Brandon, I had told him of my desire to become a doctor—a surgeon—and how having a child would make that dream impossible. I could hear the words of my stepfather in my head: "white trash" was how he thought of me. I would show him! I would make him sorry that he ever said that. I clung to that fiercely and gritted my teeth as I tried to cope with the pain. For all my book knowledge, I could not really understand what I was experiencing or what was happening. And then, after many hours, there was a sudden rush of fluid and a warm feeling in my lower parts and I felt something leave my body.

I must have fallen asleep or passed out for a few hours. When I woke up, I saw to my horror that I was still lying in the same bed in a pool of blood and mucus. Between my legs was a large mass of tissue that looked like a small baby. I started screaming.

Eventually a nurse responded to my screaming. She was very professional and quietly told me to be silent. She said, "It's a girl," as she coolly started to clean up the mess. I wondered how she could tell that the mass of bloody tissue was a girl, but I remained silent. I wanted to go to sleep again, but she insisted that everything was over and that I had to get up and get dressed. Did I have anyone to pick me up? I knew that Jim was waiting for a call to come and get me. I gave her his number. She helped me out of the bed and ordered me to get dressed. It was about thirty hours since I had first been admitted. I kept telling myself it was all over and I was free again.

When Jim picked me up, I cried on his shoulder for a long time. I felt horrible both physically and psychologically. In the back of my mind I couldn't help feeling that I had crossed a line and there was no going back, and for some reason, this made me sad. I didn't think of the baby at all because, as I kept telling myself, it wasn't actually a baby or a real person, just a "clump of cells." I pushed out of my mind the reality of the "clump of cells" I had seen lying between my legs in the hospital. I suppressed the feelings of horror I had experienced when I saw "it." I wouldn't think about it, I wouldn't.

The despondence that had come over me I naturally attributed merely to the physical ordeal and within a day or two, I was back to my "normal" self again. Life was good. I had faced an obstacle and overcome it! I was woman, HEAR ME ROAR!

The relationship with Jim went downhill fairly quickly after that. I became interested in someone who worked in the same biochemistry lab where I was working part-time at the university. Then I became interested in someone else after that. Free sex was what our generation had discovered, after all. I was now officially sexually promiscuous and proud of my liberation. I was no victim of biology! I managed to secure a prescription for birth control pills so I wouldn't have to worry about going through that hideous ordeal again. All I could think of was how unfair it was that women had to be subjected to something like getting pregnant. Men didn't have that burden! Now I understood how important it was to demand full equality with men. They had this extremely unfair biological advantage! No wonder things were so hard for women professionally. Thank God—I mean, thank *science*—for the invention of the Pill and for the amazing ability of abortion to undo our biological victimhood. I decided that when I became a doctor, I would perform abortions free of charge to any woman who wanted one. To hell with biological reality! To hell with babies and clumps of non-personhood! Women were free because of science and technology, and those were the gods I worshipped now.

For many years after that, I didn't give my abortion another thought.

Fast Forward Twenty Years

About my mid-thirties, after having been married for 6-7 years, I began to feel "my biological clock ticking," as they say. My career was on a good track; my marriage, while always rocky, seemed stable enough for the moment, and I wanted to have a child. Partly this was because friends my age already had children who were growing up before my eyes, and they seemed so enchanted with them that I wondered if the same would happen to me; but mostly, I suspect, because something in my biology (wasn't I freed from that by the Women's Movement?) was on high alert as my body began to enter the middle years.

I had been using the birth control pill since my abortion two decades before, and I unilaterally decided to stop and to see what happened—"unilaterally" meaning that I neglected to mention this decision to my husband. It took a few months, but the test I secretly bought at the local supermarket clearly indicated that I was pregnant. The next step was to tell my husband that I had stopped the Pill and that a baby was on the way. I thought he'd be thrilled. He wasn't.

Instead he was angry that I hadn't discussed it with him, since he had made it pretty plain when we married that he did not want to bring children into this screwed-up world. He had been married and divorced prior to our marriage, and I completely agreed with him about the idea of not having children—then. In my usual selfish manner, I only knew that I had changed my mind and didn't really care whether he had or not. However, I abjectly apologized for not informing him. I had not even been sure that I *could* get pregnant, after the abortion and after using the Pill for so many years.

Over time, he came around and eventually decided it was probably a good thing to have a child before we became too old. I was thrilled at the idea of becoming a mother. Who would have guessed? Certainly not me. So we began preparations for a third member of the family.

At about four months, I started to bleed. We rushed to the doctor who placed me on complete bed rest, presumably for the rest of the pregnancy. It was a daunting prospect, but I dutifully took off work and remained in bed, lying almost flat. If this was what I had to do to have a baby, then I would do it. Most of the days that followed I watched baseball (we were living in Houston at the time, so I was an Astros fan, even though my first love was and always will be the Yankees). In those days you could only access on TV the teams that played in your neck of the woods. But I was happy just to be able to watch the games, which soothed me greatly. There was also plenty of time for me to spend with my own thoughts, lying in bed with nothing much to do but read or watch TV; and quite naturally, some of those thoughts drifted back to my experience having the abortion. I'm not sure that I felt regret or anything remotely like it, but I did start thinking that I might have had a daughter who would be in her twenties now. What a fascinating thought! I wondered what she would have been like. I wondered how the father of that child was doing in his life. I had not had contact with Jim for many years. I hoped he was well. I remembered the pain and misery of the actual abortion procedure in great detail. I suspected, based on how common abortions had become and how acceptable they were now, that women were probably having an easier time getting them. I remembered that one of my friends at the time I had an abortion had been sent to Japan by her parents to have an abortion, since it had been easier to obtain one there. Now in the U.S. it was an absolute right for women to have them; it was one of the fundamental tenets of a major political party that nothing should exist to impede a woman's "right to choose." Any thoughts about what a woman was "choosing" when she deliberately set about killing her unborn child because it was inconvenient were still far from my mind, but the defenses I had built up were starting to crumble, I think.

As I reflected on all this, I rubbed the small mound of my abdomen which was just beginning to show. Somehow, the thought of the daughter that was never born made me feel deeply sad. I remembered writing a poem after the abortion, when I had rashly decided not to have children so that nothing could stand in the way of my career. I called it "To My Daughters Unborn," and I hoped the child I was carrying now within me would be a daughter. I searched through the boxes of my old notebooks looking for the poem, but it was packed away somewhere and stored in the garage.

It wasn't great poetry, perhaps, but remembering some of the words made me cry. My husband attributed my emotionality to the hormones of the pregnancy and counseled me to ignore it. He was very practical that way. But I found it hard to relate to the 17-year-old Pat who had written a poem like that, especially considering my current circumstances. I told myself very firmly that I was in total control and it had been my choice and there was no use going back and crying over what had been done. I was a liberated woman, after all.

About the middle of the fifth month of my pregnancy, I began to bleed again, even while lying down, and this time I was having bad cramping too. The pain was quite intense. I was scared and yelled at my husband to call the doctor. He dithered around for a while but finally got the doctor on the phone. I started screaming loudly that I was having the baby and the doctor said to bring me to the emergency room. I could barely move since I was in so much pain, so my husband had to carry me to the car and when we got to the hospital, he had to carry me from the car to the ER.

I don't remember much after that. My gynecologist appeared at some point and told me softly that I was losing the baby and that he was going to have to sedate me. "No! No!" I cried, "I can't be losing it." Hadn't I done all that he'd said? Couldn't they still keep the baby alive?

"I'm almost certain the baby is already dead," he said gently, and I passed out. When I awoke about four or five hours later, I was no longer pregnant. This time it had been a boy.

A profound depression settled over me. I was exhausted and tired, but I especially felt ashamed. I knew deep down that I was being punished for the abortion; and I knew that I richly deserved whatever punishment the universe doled out to me. I lay listless in the hospital bed until I was discharged the next day; and thus I remained for the next month or two. Frankly, I'm surprised that one of my colleagues didn't recommend I see a psychiatrist. But the truth was that no one talked about it much. Some female friends told me their miscarriage stories about how they lost their first or second child in spontaneous abortions or miscarriages. It happens a lot, they informed me. Their stories did not help much as I suspect what I was really finally mourning was the abortion I had had when I was 17 years old.

I was determined to get pregnant again. What followed over the next three years was me getting pregnant, then suffering spontaneous abortion after spontaneous abortion. Eight weeks; 9 weeks; 12 weeks. After the third one, I conceded to myself that I had failed to make up for the life I had taken. I was not going to be a mother after all. For the next year, I concentrated on my work at NASA as a flight surgeon in the Shuttle Program; and soon afterward I left that job to take a faculty position in psychiatry at the University of Texas Medical Branch in Galveston. About my departure from NASA, it was said that I had left to follow the "mommy-track," but I already knew that that path was closed to me.

One day while in my office at UTMB, my secretary buzzed me to let me know that Richard, my gynecologist, was on the line. "Pat," he said, "I have this 19 year old woman in my office who is having some difficulties." I started to take notes, assuming he was referring a case to me. "She is almost 4 months pregnant and she wants to give the baby up for adoption, and I thought of you because she looks like you."

That was all it took. I burst into tears. My secretary came running to find out what was wrong and I could hardly speak, I was sobbing so loudly. I remember telling the doctor, "Yes! Yes! Let me call you back in a few, I can't speak now. But definitely, yes. I will do it. However you want to work it out, I will do it."

I can't describe all that was going through my mind at that moment. I felt redeemed. I felt as if a great weight had been lifted. I felt like my life was going to be normal again, something it hadn't been for many years; not since…. I couldn't face it then, but I realize now, looking backwards, that I had deliberately interrupted my life and bought into something very wrong. I didn't connect it to my lack of faith at the time—that would come later—but this was definitely a religious experience for me: to be told, when all of my hope was gone, that I was going to be a mother after all.

My daughter was born immediately after my forty-second birthday. My husband and I paid for all the medical care of the biological mother, and I followed her closely during the pregnancy. She had been three months pregnant when Dr. Richard contacted me, and since he and I worked together, I was able to participate in her clinic visits. I was delighted when the biological mother decided that she wanted me to deliver the child and even more thrilled when I found out it was a girl.

Blessed is the Fruit of Thy Womb

The Angel said, "Hail, full of grace, the Lord is with thee." And Mary replied after hearing his message, "Behold the handmaid of the Lord. Be it done unto me according to thy word."

How obtuse I was that I didn't realize it at the time, but I was being given a great grace. How could I have failed to see the hand of the Blessed Mother in my surprise at the news of my impending motherhood? My journey back to God was just beginning, though I didn't appreciate the Father's plan at that point in time.

My daughter was born five months later. How can I describe the joyous feeling that buoyed me over those months of expectation?

I wrote my first book, *Choosing the Right Stuff,* during that time and the acknowledgments section, I wrote my thanks to many people, including: *"My loving husband, Norman Richert; and last, but not least, my daughter, Alexandra Ann, who was born at the same time I completed this manuscript and who—for me—already has the right stuff."*

Since I was a physician with some experience delivering babies, my gynecologist, Dr. Richard, and the biological mother, Laura, both agreed that I should be the attending physician in the delivery room. And so, I was the first to see her beautiful face and the first to hold her in my arms. My husband and I took her home from the hospital the next morning and began the process of adoption. We had just made it under the wire for these kinds of adoptions. The social work industry, in their wisdom (and that is sarcastic), had a cut-off age of 42 years old for couples to adopt children. I was 41 years old, and though I had thought I had missed my chance, I was now a mother!

I imagine that Mary of Nazareth must have felt something similar. Her circumstances were, shall we say, more consistent with God's plan from the beginning; but imagine her surprise as an avowed virgin to find out that she would carry the Messiah, the Son of God, in her womb. She was, without doubt, "blessed…among all women" for this greatest of honors; but, so was I now blessed beyond all reason and justice after I had chosen the path of death and selfishness, and after I had accepted that I was never going to be able to be a mother. Mary chose life and followed God's will and not her own, the ultimate unselfishness. I was the most undeserving of sinners to be blessed with a child after my cold-hearted behavior. My age was not an excuse. I had bought into the anti-Mary spirit that dominated women at the time, and I had all the information I needed to choose life and should have known better.

One of Mary's many titles in the Catholic Church is *Our Lady of Guadalupe.* Under that title, she is considered the Protector of the Unborn. Our Lady appeared to Juan Diego, a poor Mexican peasant in 1531:

> A poor Indian named Cuauhtlatohuac was baptized and given the name Juan Diego. He was a 57-year-old widower, and lived in a small village near Mexico City. On Saturday morning December 9, 1531, he was on his way to a nearby *barrio* to attend Mass in honor of Our Lady.
>
> Juan was walking by a hill called Tepeyac when he heard beautiful music like the warbling of birds. A radiant cloud appeared, and within it stood an Indian maiden dressed like an Aztec princess. The lady spoke to him in his own language and sent him to the bishop of Mexico, a Franciscan named Juan de Zumarraga. The bishop was to build a chapel in the place where the lady appeared.
>
> Eventually the bishop told Juan to have the lady give him a sign. About this same time Juan's uncle became seriously ill. This led poor Juan to try to avoid the lady. Nevertheless the lady found Juan, assured him that his uncle would recover, and provided roses for Juan to carry to the bishop in his cape or tilma.
>
> On December 12, when Juan Diego opened his tilma in the bishop's presence, the roses fell to the ground, and the bishop sank to his knees. On the tilma where the roses had been appeared an image of Mary exactly as she had appeared at the hill of Tepeyac.[10]

The image on the tilma of Juan Diego is amazing, especially in that it totally resonated with the Aztec people of the 16th century, who were very resistant to conversion from their pagan, baby-sacrificing culture to that of Christianity, brought by the Catholic missionaries: first of all, the Madonna appears as a *mestizo,* with the complexion of a person of combined Mexican and Spanish heritage. She is humble, with downcast eyes and hands clasped in prayer. Both of these postures indicated to the Aztecs that she was not a god. However, the ribbon of her tunic demonstrates that she is pregnant and her pregnant form eclipses the rays of the sun behind her, which said to the Aztecs that her child would eclipse their sun god.

---

10 https://www.franciscanmedia.org/our-lady-of-guadalupe/

*The tilma of Our Lady of Guadalupe
at the Shrine in Mexico City.*

Her tunic has four-petal flowers on it, and microscopic analysis, done fairly recently, clearly shows the petal has a baby within. Additional microscopic analysis of her eyes reveals the images of the people to whom Juan Diego brought her message and the roses. Finally, her blue-turquoise mantle displays the stars exactly as they would have appeared in the sky on the date of her apparition.

The tilma, made as it was from the fibers of a cactus common in the area, should have only lasted twenty or so years at most. Yet, 500 years later, the image is still vibrant and unmarred, despite having gone through many years without any protection and several attempts by anti-Catholics to destroy it.

The appearance of Our Lady brought an end to the cruel and barbaric human sacrifice in the Americas which was taking place at an unprecedented scale never before seen in human history. Some experts have estimated that the Aztecs sacrificed up to 250,000 children and adults annually to their gods.

Their pagan sacrifice is now mirrored in our own culture's practice and celebration of abortion: the sacrifice of human babies to the gods of progress and self-fulfillment.

It is for this reason today that Our Lady of Guadalupe is called, in addition to "Empress of the Americas," the "Patroness of the Unborn." Like the Aztec culture of the 1500s when she appeared, America has annually killed up to 1 million babies a year—60 million since Roe v. Wade was decided in 1973. These statistics are not inflated but come directly from the Guttmacher Institute, a pro-choice organization which keeps date on the number of abortions performed annually. (https://checkyourfact.com/2018/07/03/fact-check-60-million-abortions/)

This brief synopsis does not do the image justice. It is spectacular and miraculous. Today the tilma Our Lady left Juan Diego hangs in the Basilica of Guadalupe near Mexico City, and one of the first pilgrimages I made after coming back to God was to Guadalupe (see Chapter 8).

Prayer to Mary for Expectant Mothers

Humble Mary of Nazareth, you were chosen by God to bear within
you our world's greatest gift, the Savior of all humanity. I come
to you now on behalf of (here mention name) who prays for the
health and safety of the child that God has graced her to conceive.
Guard this life that God has created, and protect the mother God
has chosen for this child. Let your gentle hands, like that of a
skilled physician, assist in her delivery so that this baby will know
good health and lasting happiness.
May her child be favored with the grace of Holy Baptism, and
grow to love our Lord Jesus Christ above all else in this world.
Amen.

CHAPTER 4

WHAT GOD HAS JOINED TOGETHER

To HHT

Nothing is known
Too soon or too slowly.
We move through the day
Remaining each only.
You look and I glance;
We see the same thing,
But not the other, not you and I.

All our time passes
Too soon or too slowly,
Encompassing me with all the potential.
Whatever we have
We had and it's over.
If nothing was there,
And nothing was known,
Which love was wasted?
Yours…or my own?

Marriage

I mentioned my marriage previously, and now it's time to focus on that piece of my puzzle. It is one of the bigger pieces, as it spanned more than twenty-seven years of my life. Not unexpectedly, I suppose, after witnessing the travesty of my parents' marriage and its aftereffects on my brothers and myself, I was not a big fan of marriage; nor was I properly prepared emotionally for being a wife. I was in no hurry to get married, but strangely I yearned for a committed relationship, for "true love" and "happily ever after" and a "soulmate." I became involved in a number of sequential relationships, all of which ended badly, leaving me brokenhearted and miserable. Then in my late twenties, someone I had been fond of in high school re-entered my life out of the blue and after a brief courtship, we married.

What can I say of my marriage? It had many joys, but equally many sorrows; led to several extramarital affairs on my part (one being purely "virtual"); and was also the source of the greatest delight of my life—my daughter Alexandra. Considering her, I cannot regret the marriage, but I do feel a justified sense of shame and disappointment in myself, because I should have known better and tried harder to make it work. I am so grateful that despite my behavior and lack of commitment, my regrets and bad actions, that the Lord of the Universe was still willing to stand by me and send His Mother to lead me home again.

I say that I should have known better. What I mean by this is that, on some level, I always knew what was right and what was wrong, but that I suppressed that knowledge because it was convenient—oh so convenient—to pretend that what was wrong was good, simply because it felt good. That was the motto of the era: Do what feels good, and therefore if it feels right, it must be right! And I found it easy to follow my feelings, override my (always nagging) conscience and simply pursue pleasure. I may have told myself that I was rational and scientific or that I was basically a "good" person, but I was neither because I wasn't really thinking for myself; I was following the rules that a decadent culture proclaimed I should follow and allowing my emotions of the moment to cloud my intellect—I, who ostensibly valued intellect and mind above anything else! If I had thought about it in terms of my soul, I would have realized that I was sacrificing my soul on the altar of the new idol of the age: the self. We have a term for this kind of worship in psychiatry: *narcissism*.

"Narcissism" is a term coined by Sigmund Freud, who named the phenomenon after Narcissus in Greek mythology. Narcissus was a handsome young man who rejected the desperate advances of the nymph Echo who loved him. As a punishment, the gods doomed him to fall in love with his own reflection in a pool of water. Unable to consummate his love, Narcissus pined away and changed into the flower that bears his name. (Incidentally, Echo also wasted away until she was just a whisper, barely heard.) The clinical syndrome of narcissism is called Narcissistic Personality Disorder (NPD) and it is described in detail in *The Diagnostic and Statistical Manual of Mental Disorders* of the *American Psychiatric Association DSM-5* as "a pervasive pattern of grandiosity (in fantasy or behavior), need for admiration, and lack of empathy." According to the DSM-5, the disorder begins by early adulthood and is indicated by the subject exhibiting at least five of the following:

- A grandiose sense of self-importance

- A preoccupation with fantasies of unlimited success, power, brilliance, beauty, or ideal love

- A belief that he or she is special and unique and can only be understood by, or should associate with, other special or high-status people or institutions

- A need for excessive admiration

- A sense of entitlement

- Interpersonally exploitive behavior

- A lack of empathy

- Envy of others or a belief that others are envious of him or her

- A demonstration of arrogant and haughty behaviors or attitudes

In a proposed alternative model cited in *DSM-5,* NPD is characterized by moderate or greater impairment in personality functioning, manifested by characteristic difficulties in 2 or more of the following 4 areas:

- Identity

- Self-direction

- Empathy

- Intimacy

Typical behaviors of NPD are both grandiosity and attention seeking.[11]

Every individual has some narcissistic traits, and a certain amount of narcissism is necessary and healthy to be able to live one's life effectively. What's different about the personality disorder is that the symptoms are prominent and persistent over time and pervade every aspect of the person's existence. It can be very disabling in extreme cases, and those who exhibit this personality can make the people around them thoroughly miserable because of their manipulative, predatory and frequently un-empathic behavior. Narcissists are notoriously spiteful and vicious and usually alienate anyone emotionally close to them. They are not extreme like sociopaths or antisocial personality disorders, since a narcissist is capable of relating to others and can experience empathy.

In this day and age, narcissism—as well as sociopathy—occurs in epidemic proportions. All over the world, on a daily basis, we see the results of narcissistic behavior. Individuals and groups, religions and nations act out their narcissistic rage at various insults—real and imagined—and people suffer and die for grandiose fantasies of a tyrant, or for the glory of a religion or ideology. It has been said that the 20th century was the "century of the narcissist," but the 21st is well on its way to outdoing the horrors of the past as we face a seeming epidemic of malignant narcissism and sociopathy brought about by a culture that has declared God dead and celebrates.

Today's feminist movement, with their vagina hats and exhibitionist proclivities, is clearly rooted in narcissism, since it is no longer about equal opportunity for women, but about envy, resentment and weaponized victimhood. This is the weapon of a humanity-hating ideology. But what about victimhood, you ask? How can something like being a victim connect to narcissism? First, it is important

---

11 *Diagnostic and Statistical Manual of the American Psychiatric Association DSM-5* (2013). American Psychiatric Press. Washington D.C., pp.669-70.

to realize that there are genuine victims in the world; but feminist ideology has defined womanhood as perpetual victimhood. They fail to see any differences between males and females and insist that all the problems suffered by women are due to the "oppressive (white) male patriarchy."

Consider that the flip side of "selfish" or "grandiose" narcissism is *narcissism rooted in idealism rather than in selfishness,* or "idealistic" narcissism. This version of narcissism (the flip side of the coin, if you will) is less obvious to an observer, since it is disguised with a veneer of concern for others. But it is equally—if not more—destructive and causative of human suffering, death and misery. Both kinds of narcissism are a plague on the world, and both are well-traveled political avenues for limiting freedom and imposing tyranny. The "grandiose" narcissism is the stimulus for individual tyrants, while the "idealistic" narcissism leads to groups imposing their will on others.

Both varieties of narcissism can exist in a single person, who often vacillates from one extreme to the other. I certainly was not immune to this emphasis on the joys of entitlement or the need for excessive admiration or fame that is ubiquitous in American culture. Just think of all the self-help, self-esteem and self-actualization taglines in the articles of pop magazines, business courses, and relationship guides. The 60s and 70s gave birth to an entire industry of glorified Me-ism. *"If it feels good, do it,"* was the working standard of behavior; and this phrase is also the motto of most sociopaths and tyrants.

If I had really had the psychological insight I often give myself credit for, I should have seen the red flags that were waving right at the start of my marriage to Norm when I stubbornly insisted that I would not take his last name after we were married. I argued that I was an independent woman, a physician and psychiatrist in my own right, and that all my professional documents were in my own name and that I was proud of my name and didn't want to change it, thank you very much. This was the clearest indication that I was, from the start, unwilling to truly merge my identity in the communion of love that marriage requires. When Norm and I reconnected prior to marrying, I terminated my analytic psychotherapy because I believed that my emotional vulnerabilities had been adequately uncovered and healed. How wrong I was!

Norm was very disappointed in my decision about the name. I proposed a hyphenated name, which was popular at the time, but he declined, and so we entered the married life not as one, but as two separate individuals each with his or her own separate name, profession, and life plan. Norm felt some awkwardness at this, and in retrospect he was justified. I reassured him that this was a new day and age, where women were the equal of men, and marriage was just a convenience and did not mean that we had to actually give up anything for the other person. I pointed out to him that he should feel proud of the fact that he was a "modern man." There was to be no distribution of household duties based on gender—no stereotypical roles in this relationship! As for childcare duties, neither of us was interested at that point (we were in our late 20s) in actually having children, so it was a moot point. He was only interested in completing his PhD, and I had my grandiose professional plans of becoming a psychiatrist and astronaut and working for NASA.

With regard to NASA and becoming an astronaut, Norm humored me, never thinking for an instant that I would follow through on something so ridiculous. I was a resident in psychiatry at Harbor/UCLA Medical Center at the time of our marriage, and he was teaching mathematics at Biola University and finishing his doctorate in mathematics from Claremont Graduate School.

I had known Norm since high school, when we were both in the same "honors" English class with an incredible teacher, Mr. Robert Bell, who was probably the primary person encouraging me in my desire for an professional career. He critiqued and applauded my poetry and other writings and believed that I had some talent, which generally compensated for my self-doubt and poor self-esteem under my stepfather's roof. Norm and I had "sort of" dated back then, though because of his Mennonite background, dating was frowned on. Most of our interactions took place within a large group of fellow students, most of whom were from Mr. Bell's English class. Norm was the organizer of a group of us that came to be known as "UMBRA," and our hallmark activity was acting out various intellectual pranks and showing the rest of the school how smart we were. In my usual arrogance, I thought that since I was the smartest female in the honors class, I should date the smartest male.

This class itself was rather unique. We studied the world religions and read classic English and Greek books. We analyzed the *Lord of the Rings* by Tolkien, which was extremely popular at the time and which inspired us to take on roles from the book. I became Arwen and Norm was Aragorn. We went as these characters to our class Tolkien Masquerade Party. The pervasive influence of this class on both of us was exemplified by the fact that from that day, Norm and I always named our cars from Tolkien's trilogy: his was always BILBO, and mine was always ARWEN. (To this day, the CA license plate on my Honda Odyssey is ARWEN2).

The influence of that high school class continued for many years and expressed itself in my love of literature, poetry and reading. Tolkien became a favorite of mine. Years later I found out that he was a devout Catholic and had included much religious/Christian symbolism in his work.

We graduated from high school and tearfully said goodbye to each other since Norm was going to a Christian college near Chicago—Wheaton—which was a tradition in his family, as almost every child had matriculated there for the last several generations. I, on the other hand,was going to the local UC Riverside, since I could not afford to go elsewhere. For a few months, we kept in regular touch via letters. Norm always ended his letters with "May the hair on your toes grow ever longer," an affectionate phrase from *The Hobbit.* We even played chess by mail. But I was disappointed because he didn't write to me as if he was in love, only as a person who thought of me as a friend, and my hormones demanded more. In college, I dated quite a bit, and finally one of the guys who was on the periphery of our UMBRA group became my official boyfriend.

Norm was shocked and hurt at Thanksgiving when I told him that I couldn't go out with him since I was seeing Jim. He walked away and did not look back or speak to me again for almost ten years. I learned shortly thereafter that he went back to Wheaton and proposed to someone and that they were getting married. Needless to say, I was not invited, and I was a little hurt that Norm refused to have anything to do with me or even speak to me after he found out that I was dating someone else—even though we had never officially "dated," nor had he even kissed me, even when we said goodbye before leaving for college. Apparently, he felt such things as words were not necessary for communicating his emotions. But, in truth, I was desperately needy (as most people with strong narcissistic traits are).

He contacted me one day, ten years after our last conversation, when I was in my psychiatric residency. Years had passed, but I recognized his voice on the phone right away. I knew from the moment he called, that we would get married, though I had to ask him if he was still married to the Wheaton person. He informed me that he was in the middle of a divorce and he had thought of me and got my contact information from mutual friends. Three months after making contact, we were engaged and planning on living together; six months later we had a formal wedding with all the trimmings. I believed it was another magical *Cinderella* moment—I had married the prince against the wishes of the evil stepmother, or was it stepfather?

Of course, I avoided thinking about how very different we were and focused on our early connection from high school. We actually were exact opposites, which was probably the reason we had been attracted to each other to begin with. He was calm, somewhat withdrawn, while I was more emotionally outgoing and wore my feelings on my sleeve. He was politically left and I was right; he was anti-military, from a family of pacifists; and I was gung-ho about the military. He was Mennonite, then Baptist, then Episcopal. I was a former Catholic and current atheist. He wanted me to take his last name; I refused. He wanted to live in the house he had in Pasadena; I had a great apartment in Santa Monica and would have to commute quite a distance if I lived with him. I was talkative; he was not. I had strong narcissistic traits; he had strong obsessive compulsive ones. I was looking for love, he was looking for a companion.

But the worst of our differences was made manifest shortly after we had been married for about a year. He finally completed his PhD and was looking for an academic position. I never realized before then how much he resented and was threatened by the fact that as an MD I would always make more money than he did, since he intended to only work in the academic environment. He accepted a job at Marquette University in Milwaukee, Wisconsin, but only told me about it after the fact. I felt angry and hurt. He had known that I wanted to work in the space program. I told him, in a parody of Star

Wars: "If there's a bright center to the universe, then Milwaukee is furthest from it." I refused to go to Wisconsin. We fought about it, each of us feeling betrayed by the other.

That fall he moved there and started his position. I stayed behind for a while, then finally decided that I should go there too—not out of any sense of obedience to my husband, but only because I was miserable now living by myself. I found an academic job at the University of Wisconsin in Milwaukee and moved into the apartment he had rented in a high rise downtown. I hated it—which is why he finally agreed to purchase a house in the suburbs. I loved the house, a one-story ranch with an acre of wooded land on the Milwaukee River. I could have been happy there if it were not for my ambition to become an astronaut and work for the space program.

Honestly, it was my professional ambitions and my narcissistic need to be loved and adored that ruined our marriage, though the process was a slow and painful one that took place over many more disappointments and betrayals on both our parts. NASA eventually hired me as a flight surgeon and I told him I was moving to Houston because this was my chance to be part of the space program.

Norm was shocked because he never imagined that I would ever get a job with NASA. Tit for tat, I thought privately. Without regret, I moved to Houston to begin my big adventure. In my mind, the marriage was basically over. We lived apart for over a year, and it was during this separation that I engaged in my first extramarital affair, convinced that Norm would never move to Houston and leave Wisconsin and his job at Marquette University. On his part, he felt I was ruining his career as a mathematician and indeed, my moving to Houston probably influenced the tenure committee against him becoming tenured at Marquette. Only when it was clear that he would not, in fact, get tenure, did he consider moving to Houston.

He eventually found a faculty position at the newly-opened University of Houston, Clear Lake campus, and moved down. But I was never really going to give myself wholeheartedly to the relationship again after that. I was outraged at his unwillingness to accept my career goals (it didn't occur to me that I didn't accept his) and neither of us understood the meaning of sacrifice for the sake of the other. All this rationalization at my "betrayal" by his failure to support me, led to several brief sexual liaisons on my part, but I made sure Norm didn't find out. After he moved down, we saw a marriage counselor for a year or so, and I never revealed my infidelity. We got back together, primarily because I selfishly decided I wanted to have children, even if he did not.

I didn't tell him that I was off the birth control pill and when I became pregnant, he was very angry. Tit for tat, I thought again, rather smugly. There is a saying among psychiatrists who have a certain contempt for psychoanalysis: "If you take an asshole and psychoanalyze him (or her, in my case), what you get is a well-analyzed asshole." I never imagined that the diagnosis could be applied to me.

After the multiple miscarriages, Norm finally came around to wanting children, but initially was averse to adopting a child even when it became clear that I could not carry one to term.

By the time our daughter Alexandra was born and the adoption papers signed, we had been married twelve years. I decided after her birth that Clear Lake was where I wanted to be. Though I was no longer working for NASA by then, I was working on research related to the space program and had officially given up my desire to be an astronaut and instead was involved in the NASA astronaut selection process. I was relatively content. I was not an obedient or faithful wife, but I like to think I was a good mother. From the moment Alexandra was born, I gave up working full-time and devoted myself to participating in our daughter's upbringing. I was involved at her school; our home was a center for her and her playmates; and I was happy using Norm's last name so as not to confuse her and her friends. I discovered that I felt much more fulfilled as a mother than I had ever dreamed possible in light of the feminist propaganda I had absorbed over the years. Soon, I even began to resent that I had to work outside the home. Now I was the one who was upset that I made more money as a physician than Norm did as an academic mathematician. When Alexandra was about 4 years old we had a brief separation for a few months, but came back together when I admitted that I missed him. After that, things settled down between us for a long time as we concentrated on raising our daughter.

This period of relative contentment was interrupted when Norm suddenly had an opportunity to follow his own dream. One of the well-known mathematical journals needed an assistant editor and he applied for the job, which was in Ann Arbor, Michigan. Much as I dreaded the idea of moving to that part of the country again, I proposed a bargain: I would quit my job and focus on Alexandra and the home we would have in Ann Arbor if he got the job. Those were my conditions for moving. Norm agreed. We could use my retirement funds to help us purchase a house, but we would live only on his salary. What a switch from those all-consuming and grandiose dreams of career, fortune and fame! I thought we had finally resolved the key struggles in our relationship. Once again, I was incorrect.

We moved to Ann Arbor. I was excited about not working and concentrating on child rearing. I had plans to become a Girl Scout Leader and give my daughter all the advantages I felt I didn't have as a child.

My not working lasted a mere three months before Norm demanded that I return to working as a doctor. We couldn't afford to live on his salary alone, he claimed. Not if we wanted to continue to live in the house we had bought (even though we bought it based on his salary alone). Again I felt betrayed. In many ways, I really disliked Ann Arbor. It was, as the wags would say, "ten square miles surrounded by reality." It was a very politically leftist town. You would walk down the main streets of the downtown area and could swear you were still living in the 60s. Everyone wore Birkenstocks and dressed like hippies (an exaggeration on my part, but that was the dominant ambience). All the men wore their hair long and tied back in pony tails (I exaggerate, but you get the idea). The local government was more interested in making political statements rather than actually running the city in an efficient manner, it seemed to me. Seething with resentment yet again, I went back to work part-time as a psychiatrist. I began to hate my job. Norman also hated my job, primarily because even working part-time I made so much more money as a physician than he did. He made sure I understood that he was never going to make much more than he was already making and that I would always have to work to make ends meet. What I didn't know at the time was that a big chunk of our money was going to his church. I didn't know because I let Norm handle our finances. But I could never understand why we didn't have any money to do things, especially things I wanted to do. I secretly opened a bank account in my name only and held back some of the money I was giving to Norm for our expenses. I used that money to buy myself things, because shopping made me feel better about my situation. In short, I was unhappy.

Then the World Trade Center attack happened on September 11, 2001. By that time, we had been living in Ann Arbor for almost four years. The national impact of that attack and the death toll jolted and psychologically stunned me. Never had I imagined our country could be so vulnerable. I cried for days. Norm was initially upset, then took the view that perhaps we—America—deserved it. I was even more shocked that anyone could take that position, but it seemed to be a common opinion in the Ann Arbor area, and I grew to absolutely despise the kind of thinking that lay behind such a pronouncement. I truly believe that on that day, our marriage sustained a wound from which it would never recover. Never in our relationship had the political differences been so marked, and over the next several years they just became more and more stark.

I started to blog and found solace in the conservative media. In contrast, Norm moved more to the political left. I met a blogger online with whom I seemed to have a lot in common. We began to email and skype frequently, and soon I was involved in an online "affair" that convinced me to finally file for divorce. The person I had met online during my blogging days as "Dr. Sanity" seemed to me to be the soulmate I had always been looking for. I felt that Norm did not know me, had never known me, and likely would never know who I was or approve of me. In my mind, he took on the worst aspects of those who hated our country and wanted to see it cut down to size. I was convinced he was ashamed of my opinions and of me. It didn't help that he blamed me for his being demoted at work after I had a politically heated discussion with his boss' wife.

I never met my supposed "soulmate" in person, but we carried on a steamy affair through the internet. And I became persuaded that my marriage needed to end. I suppose I had it in my mind that I would meet this person "Alex" and we would live happily ever after in total bliss. I was unbelievably stupid, and I listened uncritically to all his supportive advice and accepted his comfort.

Norm and I attempted to work it out by going to a therapist again. But I felt besieged on all sides, and my heart wasn't in the therapy. This time I wanted out. I remember once coming home from the therapist's office and crying in the car. Norm gently put his hand on my leg and for a brief moment, I softened. But then I remembered all my grievances and my heart hardened again. I was done with the marriage.

The next few months were horrible. He moved into the guest bedroom. We told our daughter, who was 15 years old and took the news very poorly. I had imagined she would not be very happy, but I wasn't prepared for her grades to deteriorate and for her behavior to become so problematic. I should have been prepared, but I wasn't. Again, I was more wrapped up in my own problems and didn't have the inclination to think about hers very much, I guess. Those kinds of problems didn't happen to me. We went to mediation, and I felt I had been screwed financially. Norm stopped speaking to me and moved out. In the year before I moved to California, he never communicated with me except through our daughter, who lived out of a suitcase, spending one week to his apartment, the next week at the house where I remained. It was very hard on her, and the ripple effects of that time impacted her greatly for many years. And then, after all that, I discovered that my online "soulmate" was a con artist. Quite by accident, I became aware that he had the same kind of relationship with multiple women bloggers, leading them all on about himself and his love and concern for them. *What a bunch of losers we all are,* I thought to myself, but I was truly devastated because my judgment had been so completely wrong about this person. I consider myself so intelligent, so sensitive, and I had been royally conned by someone into believing that he loved me. I felt like a complete idiot.

One small consolation was that one of my friends, who is a famous mystery writer, found the story of my virtual affair fascinating and wrote one of her serial detective books about what happened to me. Of course it was disguised, but the book was dedicated to me. It made me feel only marginally better for being so stupid and gullible. As she told me at the time, "You can't do anything to him, but I can kill him in my book." And she did. Quite horribly. In a way, I wished she would kill me too in that book, but the fictional me came out okay. Not so in my real life, however.

What an awful situation I had created for everyone who truly mattered to me! I began to feel a great deal of remorse and regret about my own behavior during that time. Being a child of divorce myself, I should have understood the implications for my daughter. But I was intractably selfish and only thought of my own feelings. I had also been keeping several secrets from Norm that dated back to our first separation. He never suspected anything about my affairs while I was at NASA, nor did I confess them in our marital therapy sessions because I feared he would leave me (he always promised that he would if I was unfaithful). Like a good little narcissist, I wanted to keep my options open. I didn't think of myself as an adulterer because I felt justified in my own betrayals and rationalized my behavior while at the same time denouncing his lesser transgressions. And then I was even unfaithful over the internet. Isn't technology wonderful? When was I going to grow up?

WHEN, DAUGHTER?

Ten years after we ended the marriage, I was finally honest with myself and came to a full appreciation of how much I had contributed to the demise of our family. I felt appropriate shame and abject horror at what I had done in my selfish pursuit of the modern feminism's ideal: self-actualized victimhood. I had justified my actions by believing that I was the victim—of what, I can't say, even to this day.

Do Whatever He Tells You

By now, anyone reading this is thinking that you know much more about my life than you ever wanted to know. You may even be thinking that I am not a very nice person. I understand completely. Looking back, I feel the same way. In my marriage, I was not a particularly nice or virtuous individual. In these matters and others, I was deceitful, selfish, thoughtless, and yes, narcissistic. These confessions are both painful and liberating at the same time, like ripping a Band-Aid off a wound. Somehow, these self-revelations led me to understand that God never abandoned me despite all the trespasses that I committed against Him and others. My remorse was just. I could have slid into despair, but God rescued me at exactly the perfect moment, when I was ready to finally accept His reality. He has, in His never-ending, boundless love, forgiven me; and the least I can do is to forgive everyone who has sinned against me over the years. But, as you can see, I have done more sinning against than being sinned against. The divorce was mostly my fault. We both contributed to the failure of the marriage, but it was I who left. I was not a good wife; I never knew how to be a good wife, and I never tried to find out. All I was ever concerned about was me and my own feelings. They were the gold standard in everything I did.

St. Augustine wrote, commenting on the woman caught in adultery in the Gospel of John:

> I look at the way the Lord's answer [in the Gospel reading] upheld justice without forgoing clemency. He was not caught in the snare his enemies had laid for him; it is they themselves who were caught in it. He did not say the woman should not be stoned, for then it would look as though he were opposing the law. But he had no intention of saying: "Let her be stoned," because he came not to destroy those he found but to seek those who were lost. Mark his reply. It contains justice, clemency, and truth in full measure… What is this, Lord, are you giving approval to immorality? Not at all. Take note of what follows: "Go and sin no more." You see then that the Lord does indeed pass sentence, but it is sin he condemns, not people.

> One who would have approved of immorality would have said: "Neither will I condemn you. Go and live as you please; you can be sure that I will acquit you. However much you sin, I will release you from all penalty, and from the tortures of hell and the underworld." He did not say that. He said: "Neither will I condemn you": you need have no fear of the past, but beware of what you do in the future. "Neither will I condemn you": I have blotted out what you have done; now observe what I have commanded, in order to obtain what I have promised.[12]

How could I "do whatever He told me" when I had made myself and my own voice the center of the universe? I had closed my mind, my eyes and my ears to Him.

Possibly the only thing that moved me off that center was when Norm and I adopted Alexandra. Motherhood was responsible for transporting me into experiencing real, self-sacrificing love for the first time in my life. It was because of the overwhelming love I had for my daughter that I could finally accept the world without me as the center. It was like waking up into a different reality, where I didn't have to be successful; I didn't have to be famous; I didn't

---

12 Augustine. *Homilies on the Gospel of John*, #33. Translated by F. Barnecut. Pp. 6-7.

have to be anything but myself, the mother of this beautiful, helpless child. Who knew that a person could love another person so deeply, so strongly, so…*selflessly*.

If only I had spent more time as an adult contemplating the life of Mary. She was the role model I needed all my life. While she did not suffer from the concupiscence that the rest of the human race had to deal with—that I had to deal with—since she was born without Original Sin, she was the original liberated woman. How backwards the women's movement got it all. We were not oppressed by the things they said oppressed us—like men, children, housework, or so-called "traditional" femininity. On the contrary, it was those very things in our lives that set us free to be real women and gave us the ultimate dignity in life. That seems counterintuitive, but it is not! I followed all the feminist rules: I didn't want children; my needs came first and I aborted my first child. I wanted a man in my life, not to protect and defend me, but to enjoy sex with; and when the sex seemed more interesting elsewhere, I was willing to commit adultery. I didn't enter into the sacrament of marriage to bring him or myself closer to the Lord; nor, I think, did he really marry me for that reason, either. He may have been a Christian, but I can't remember a single conversation we ever had all our years of married life that concerned God or any theological question. Yet, he had faith, while I did not.

I liked to pride myself on being a good mother, but I lacked the most essential ingredients of true motherhood, as exemplified by Mary: faith, humility and trust as a daughter of God. I subscribed to the secular belief that sees God as sexist and anti-female, so I wanted nothing to do with Him.

Much later I learned to my surprise that, on the contrary, God has always attributed equal dignity and worth to women—and even given them an irreplaceable role in salvation history.

First, throughout the Old and New Testaments of the Bible, the uniqueness of the gift of femininity has been a running theme. Consider that Eve was created from Adam's rib—not from his skull (above) or his feet (below) but from a part of his body that symbolizes equality with him. Consider the spiritual importance of the act of reproduction, in which man and woman become one flesh in a communion of love, an image that brings to mind the Holy Trinity and the *imago Dei*.

Pope John Paul II in one of his audiences that provided cat-echesis on the Virgin Mary as a model of woman's role in the con-temporary world, said:

> ...[T]he role entrusted to Mary by the divine plan of salvation sheds light on the vocation of woman in the life of the Church and society by defining its difference in relation to man. The model represented by Mary clearly shows what is specific to the femi-nine personality.
>
> In recent times some trends in the feminist movement, in order to advance women's emancipation, have sought to make her like man in every way. However, the divine intention manifested in creation, though desiring women to be man's equal in dignity and worth, at the same time clearly affirms her diversity and specific features. Woman's identity cannot consist in being a copy of man, since she is endowed with her own qualities and prerogatives, which give her a particular uniqueness that is always to be fos-tered and encouraged.[13]

John Paul goes on to describe what he considers the "natural abilities typical of women." First, there is women's unique role in the redemption of humanity. Mary's *fiat,* "Let it be done to me according to your word," is the essence of Mary's conscious and free cooperation with God to become the mother of the Savior. Her role—and women's role, by extension—is one of cooperation with her partner in creation.

Second, women have been and continue to be essential in grow-ing the Kingdom of God on earth. Though it may seem to some that women have a lesser role than that of men (who can be priests), this belief—like most of modern anti-Mary feminism—obscures the true biological, psychological and spiritual differences between men and women. Due to these natural differences their roles are different, but equally important. Men can be priests and fathers, but they can-not be mothers (notwithstanding the gender insanity that has taken over the culture in these times).

How can the Kingdom of God on earth grow without children, first nurtured and developed in the miraculous womb of women, and then after birth nurtured and formed into the next generation

---

13 John Paul II. "Mary Sheds Light on the Role of Women," December 6, 1995. https://www.EWTN.com/library/papaldoc/jp2bvm8.htm

of Christ's followers? Women are the crucible of life, an honored role given to them by the Creator of the Universe. One of the many unspeakable horrors of abortion is that it has alienated women from their own nature and encouraged them to commit a demonically-inspired version of murder/suicide.

In my own lifetime, feminists have abandoned "equal opportunity" in the culture at large as a goal, and now demand the eradication of any biological, psychological and spiritual difference between the sexes, in defiance of reality. That old meme that I once thought so amusing, has changed from "a woman without a man is like a fish without a bicycle" to "a woman is a man (and a man is a woman), just like a fish is a bicycle."

Those natural differences rationally lead to differing roles in the Kingdom, and to the simple truth that, in the eyes of God, women and men share equal worth and dignity.

Consider that from the beginning of His ministry, Jesus consistently countered the prevailing cultural bias that accepted women as inferior to men by treating all the women he interacted with as equals. He spoke to them in public (even to a Samaritan woman!); he healed a woman on the Sabbath; and He repeatedly showed marked respect, consideration, and compassion for not only his Mother, but also for other women among the disciples and among those with whom He interacted. He referred to one woman miraculously cured of her bleeding infirmity as a "daughter of Abraham"—a title showing equality with "son of Abraham."

Additionally, the story of Martha and Mary demonstrates that Jesus believed that women who participated in learning had the "better part," and He accepted women from all walks of life—even prostitution—into discipleship. In Jesus' time, women did not often leave their homes, let alone follow a rabbi and learn Scripture.

Except for John, only women were present at Jesus' Crucifixion; and it was a woman, Mary Magdalene, to whom Jesus first revealed Himself after His Resurrection.

How can we possibly imagine the Church today without the accomplishments of women? Women make up the teachers, evangelizers, mystics, martyrs, saints, and Doctors of the Church. They have been (and continue to be) the loving and devoted mothers—modeled after Mary—who formed the teachers, evangelizers, mystics, priests, bishops, popes, kings, queens, martyrs and saints of the Church for thousands of years. How can their role possibly be thought of as unimportant or lesser than that of men in the Kingdom of God, simply because they are not priests?

Our Blessed Mother, the *Theotokos,* was not a priest; yet our salvation would not have occurred without her, since it was she who was elected by God to bring Salvation into the world. God, the Omnipotent One, out of an infinite number of ways by which He could have reconciled the world to Himself, chose a *woman* through whom to accomplish it.

In the same way, Holy Mother Church grows the Kingdom of God through the differing but co-equal talents of women and men cooperating with God's Will.

In his apostolic letter *Mulieris Dignitatem*, John Paul II writes about women's dignity and uses the term *feminine genius:*

> The Church gives thanks for all the manifestations of the feminine "genius" which have appeared in the course of history, in the midst of all peoples and nations; she gives thanks for all the charisms which the Holy Spirit distributes to women in the history of the People of God, for all the victories which she owes to their faith, hope and charity: she gives thanks for all the fruits of feminine holiness.[14]

Third, only women are able to give birth and become mothers, nurturing and giving life to children:

> The figure of Mary reminds women today of the value of motherhood. In the contemporary world an appropriate and balanced importance is not always given to this value. In some cases, the need for women to work in order to provide for the needs of their family and an erroneous concept of freedom, which sees childcare as a hindrance to woman's autonomy and opportunities, have obscured the significance of motherhood for the development of the feminine personality. On the contrary, in other cases the biological aspect of childbirth becomes so important as to overshadow the other significant opportunities woman has for expressing her innate vocation to being a mother.[15]

14 Pope John Paul II. Apostolic Letter *Mulieris Dignitatum: On the Dignity and Vocation of Women,* August 15, 1988.

15 Ibid.

Interestingly, in the world of today, we see that even as women have demanded to have all the privileges of men, they now must deal with the farcical and bizarre attempts of the transgender movement that supports men usurping women's roles and experiences, not because they are biologically suited for such activities, but because science can fit them into a diabolical procrustean bed and make them "fake women." If there is nothing special about being a woman, if even a man can have babies and fake vaginas, then why all the fuss about "women's rights"?

When I was a very young woman, I confidently left home to make my fortune. Along the way, I gave almost everything up that really mattered in life in order to achieve success. As a daughter of God, I disavowed my Father and, taking my talent and intellect and love—my entire inheritance from God—I squandered it all in loose living and pleasure, pursuing selfish desires and self-fulfillment by emphasizing how I could do anything a man could do. Yes, I could be a doctor, pilot jet planes, be a leader and assertive, etc. etc. But so what? What did that gain me? A few moments of pleasure? An overweening arrogance that I was smarter than everyone else?

All the while, the one thing I could do that men could not, I completely rejected. As a fair imitation of a man, I did OK, but just think how great I might have been as a real woman! Women like me always complained that men didn't like "strong women." That was our excuse for failed relationships and unhappy lives. We expected the men to change. But we were really imitation men, not strong women, and we rejected good men simply because we considered them "beneath us" intellectually and professionally. No wonder we were so miserable! Real men don't want to plan a life with imitation men. In a sense, by swallowing the whole feminist ideology, we set ourselves up for the transgender insanity that now pervades progressivism.

And now it is fitting and divinely ironic (as well as probably diabolical) that transgendered, imitation women are beating real women in sports, winning beauty contests over real women, and even proclaiming the right to have babies. Is it any surprise that the usurpation of womanhood follows the toxic feminine usurpation of real manhood?

Our Lady,
Undoer of Knots.

St. Thomas Aquinas says that we all try to find happiness, but unfortunately, we humans often haven't a clue as to how to go about it. I wanted freedom to be myself, but the disastrous freedom I embraced only led to recriminations and regret. The misuse of the freedom that is given to us by God always leads to the consequences I faced in my own life. And, I am certainly not the only woman duped by the feminist fantasy.

I misused my freedom to enter into the anti-God, anti-Mary movement of toxic femininity. I misused that freedom to exercise my sexual "liberty" and misused my freedom to kill my own child, and to betray a man I had vowed to "love, honor and obey" for the rest of my life. But what did such promises mean to a "liberated" woman like myself? Not much, as you can see. I was married to a decent, hard-working man who never physically abused me, and we had a beautiful daughter we both delighted in. Whatever his faults, he didn't deserve a wife who was unfaithful in mind as well as body. Good Lord! I had become my mother without consciously trying. I thought I had rejected the model of my earthly mother, but instead I unwittingly copied her! If only I had had the insight and courage to model myself after my spiritual mother.

Worst of all, I had misused my freedom to mock the God who made me free. I was slowly beginning to understand that if you are determined to leave God out of your life and turn your back on Him, then life is not going to go well for you. Yes, I was relatively materially well-off, established, and well-regarded in my profession. I should have been happy, but I was still selfish and needy, and there was still a gaping hole in my heart that ached constantly. Would nothing ever fill it? Becoming a mother myself was the first step on the long road to healing and to accepting the love of my spiritual mother. When I prayed her rosary, it was always a light on the path back to her Son, who with the Father in heaven loved me unconditionally. All God wanted was for me to return home to Him.

WHEN, DAUGHTER?

Not yet…not yet….

A Prayer to Mary, Undoer of Knots

Blessed Mother, take into your hands the knots that affect married
couples, and with your long fingers of love and grace, undo
these knots for the glory of God. Visit married couples with your
grace, renew their sacramental covenant, increase God's love
in them, and strengthen their bond of peace so that, with their
children, they may always rejoice in the gift of your blessing.
Mary, Undoer of Knots, pray for us.

CHAPTER 5

THE JOURNEY OUT AND IN

Transit of Earth

From this lonely outpost
I see a blue-green haze,
floating through a raging blaze,
stirring my soul's ghost.

The color of your eyes,
staring past the vacuum sea,
looking wistfully at me.
Burning in the sun's passion, hope dies.

I shiver in the cold.
My hands reach out to touch—
I didn't want to feel this much.
You disappear to nothing I can hold.

My frozen planet suits me well.
I long for Earth and wait till when
you pass across the sun again,
and I escape this icy hell.

Spacemen and Poets

Can spacemen fall in love in space?
Can they kiss, can they embrace?
Will love last long at speeds of light?
Can it survive an endless night?

Will poets ever walk on Mars?
Or write to Earth from dying stars?
Will life be better or be worse
When we rhyme the universe?

The Final Frontier?

A major coping mechanism in my youth while my parents' marriage was breaking down was my escape into science fiction and the excitement of space exploration. I gobbled up Asimov, Heinlein and many other authors in my enthusiasm for exploring the "final frontier." I was good at science as well as English and went back and forth in my mind as to which would be the direction I would go. I was, in my own mind at least, a poet and writer, but the lure of the vast outer darkness thrilled me, and the thought of being one of the first to adventure into that mysterious void was terribly stimulating.

It also filled a deep psychological need to escape from the awfulness of my home environment and to focus on something beyond myself, God no longer being something/someone I permitted myself to think about. Of course, the usual reaction by adults and teachers to my dream of becoming an astronaut and journeying into space, was a polite pat on the head followed by, "That's nice. Good luck." No one actually believed I would follow this path.

In college many of my geeky friends and I were obsessed with *Star Trek*, a new TV series, and we waited with high anticipation for each week's episode. The three main characters were Captain James T. Kirk, First Lt. Spock and Doctor Leonard McCoy, ship's surgeon. Most of my friends were totally into Kirk or Spock, both of whose characters I admired; but I wanted to be Dr. McCoy. I had thought in high school about the possibility of becoming a doctor, and it appealed to me a great deal; and it was in college that this thought became real and attached to the other desire to go into space. I started to plan my courses around going to medical school. I knew that I wanted to work with a Captain Kirk, to have that kind of leader in charge. I never wanted to be the leader, but I yearned to follow a fearless leader and perform heroic acts. In fact, I had a schoolgirl crush on the character of Captain Kirk which persisted for many years and along with catastrophic interactions with my father and stepfather, probably fueled my deep disappointment and unhappiness with most of my relationships with men. Somewhere along the way, I morphed into a female version of Captain Kirk myself, since I never found a man like him in real life, even within the ranks of the astronauts when I first became a flight surgeon at NASA.

I was accepted to several California medical schools and decided to go to UCLA as I could afford the move to Los Angeles from Riverside where I was in college. I had majored in biochemistry and English and Greek literature and minored in philosophy and economics. There was no subject that did not interest me in college and I soaked up every topic like a sponge.

This intellectualization was comforting and was yet another defense mechanism against the deep insecurity and sadness I carried around inside me, but it was also a very effective means of coping and I was not too excessively neurotic, I think, except possibly in my numerous unsuccessful relationships with men over the years. The UCLA School of Medicine was not at all what I imagined it to be when I began classes there. I had, in my narcissistic way, believed that I would be among "la crème de la crème," but the truth was that medical school was much less challenging than college had been, and the courses primarily involved a lot of memorization and not a lot of thinking or abstract thought of any kind. Some of the silliest and most dogmatic people I met were doctors. Many of them somewhat hostile to women being in the profession, especially to women who wanted to become surgeons, like I did.

One specific incident during those four unhappy years remains very clear in my mind. During my surgery rotation, I was supposed to scrub in for an abdominal surgery and arrived only to find that there were no scrub dresses (women medical students were supposed to wear scrub dresses like the nurses in those days) available. I hastily peeked into the doctor's dressing room and seeing no one there, grabbed a pair of scrub pants and a shirt, then got dressed and hastened to the operation I was assisting in.

What happened next is hard for anyone these days to believe, but the main surgeon noticed right away that I was not wearing a scrub *dress* and demanded that I leave the operating room immediately. He had the head nurse and security escort me out and informed me that I could kiss my residency in surgery goodbye if I persisted in breaking the "rules."

Initially, I was utterly humiliated, then angry. I immediately consulted a lawyer and hit the research library. It turned out that the US lagged behind many other countries in the practice of using surgical scrub *dresses* in the operating room. There were many articles proving that persons wearing such dresses were the source of operating room contamination from "between the legs." Scrub pants were recommended for both men and women. Armed with legal and scientific arguments, I confronted the Department Chair, who was a well-known surgeon. The upshot was that I made my point and from that time on, both men and women were instructed to wear scrub pants. However, the Chair took a dim view of being lectured by a mere girl and informed me that my rebellious attitude would ensure that I would not get into a surgical program if he had anything to do with it.

At that stage, it didn't much matter to me. I no longer had any desire to be a surgeon. I had observed many surgeons by that time and it was clear to me that I did not fit into that particular club. I searched around for what other specialty I might fit into with my diverse interests. Unexpectedly, I discovered that I liked psychiatry. There was an aura of mystery about it and it seemed like the field was on the verge of many scientific breakthroughs in understanding not only the brain, but also the mind. Also, I had two powerfully emotional experiences, one in my third year of school and one in my fourth year.

In the third-year surgical ward rotation, I was assigned to a team with a senior resident, a junior resident and another medical student. The senior resident was an amazing person who was quite charismatic. He was the sort of person, I remember thinking, who could keep patients alive by the force of his personality alone. James would tell them, while looking directly into their eyes with sincerity and confidence, that they were going to be OK. And they would get better. Even people in distress in the ICU would calm down when he put his hands on their shoulders and spoke to them. I was enthralled with his ability to *heal*, not just with his technical expertise or general surgical knowledge, which were superior.

During the six-week rotation, I don't remember a single patient expiring on his watch. But when he left the unit for his next rotation, all hell broke loose. Patients who were thought to be stable crashed and coded. Other staff said that his personality had "held them together." Did I mention that James was deeply religious? I can't recall the specifics because I wasn't into that sort of thing, but he wore a cross and often prayed with his patients. I tucked this experience away into my mind for future analysis.

The second experience was with one of the surgical patients I was caring for in my fourth year surgical rotation, shortly after the operating room fiasco. It was my interaction with this patient which basically changed my life's trajectory.

She was a woman in the end stages of breast cancer, perhaps in her mid to late fifties. I noticed that when the surgical team went on rounds they would never enter her room, but discuss her case briefly outside it. She had come into the hospital for some exploratory surgery and it was discovered during the procedure that she had cancer all over. The consensus was that she had very little time left to live. The surgeons had closed her up, told her the prognosis and because of all the laboratory abnormalities, kept her in hospital awaiting her imminent death.

Apparently she had no close relatives and did not receive any visitors. Curious, I decided on my off time to visit her. I found a remarkably cheerful lady, delighted to talk to me about any topic. It turned out that she was a published poet and had led a very interesting life. Her name was Mary, and I found that I could talk with her about the operating room incident and have a sympathetic listener. She told me about her life and read me her poems, which I enjoyed very much. She was like a breath of fresh air in a decaying alley. My visits with her delighted me, and in a relatively short time I knew her life story intimately. I started visiting her every day after my work on the ward was done and before I left for home.

One day about five weeks later, the team didn't even bother to stop outside her room on rounds. "What about Mrs. C?" I asked. I was peremptorily informed by the chief resident that Mrs. C had died early that morning.

The effect this announcement had on me was unexpected. I fled from rounds after making some excuse. Totally distraught, I went home, then went to the beach nearby to think. I was completely devastated that Mary had died. I was angry because I felt that no one on the team really cared that she had died. She had been written off when they could no longer surgically treat her cancer. I asked myself, did I want this kind of life? Hadn't I done more to help Mary just by talking to her regularly and getting involved with her life? It didn't occur to me that Mary had helped me probably more than I had helped her. And then a strange thought entered my mind: maybe I should consider psychiatry as a specialty. I had enjoyed the brief rotation we students had on the psychiatric unit. It didn't necessarily appeal to my scientific instincts, but I enjoyed talking to the patients in psychiatry and they were fascinating; the mind was fascinating. When I entered medical school, if you had asked me what specialties I was considering, psychiatry would have been dead last on the list. But the idea did not go away and only became more persistent as my fourth year was ending.

I decided to apply to only one psychiatry residency as it was already too late to participate in the Match Program, which matched medical students with programs in their specialty requests. I was accepted into the rotating internship program with an emphasis on psychiatry at UCLA Harbor Medical Center. Classmates expressed concern that I would consider such a specialty, since psychiatry was not considered "scientific" or held in high esteem by many other specialties. My boyfriend at the time, a fellow med student in my class, expressed how disappointed in me he was. He had matched at UCLA in Internal Medicine. He had also started secretly dating a first year medical student behind my back, and ultimately broke up with me before either of our residencies started.

Four years of medical school ended, and it was possibly one of the low points of my life. I was all alone again; I was rejected by someone I thought I loved; and I had grave reservations about my decision to pursue psychiatry. How would I ever get to space as a psychiatrist? Would the space program want someone with that kind of background? I reasoned that surely a psychiatrist would be useful for space exploration. I started to look up articles on psychological aspects of space flight and astronaut selection and was somewhat consoled.

In my first year of residency I shared my enthusiasm for space with two of my fellow residents. One was in internal medicine, Anna; and the other was her boyfriend, Bill, a surgical resident. My "rotating" internship had me spending 1-2 months each on medicine, ER, surgery and OB as well as in the psychiatric ward the first year. The three of us became good friends and spent a lot of time talking about space exploration and NASA. At the end of the first year, which was also the first year the Agency opened up selection to mission specialists as well as pilots, both Anna and Bill applied for the position of astronaut at NASA. I did not apply, since I reasoned that I should finish out the residency to be able to have something to offer NASA. Much to my amazement—and theirs—Anna was accepted as one of the first women to be selected for astronaut training. Bill and I were jubilant—but in all honesty, I had mixed feelings. Why hadn't I applied?. I remember a celebration dinner we had at a local Indian restaurant. Bill was determined to move with her to Houston, and they decided to get married, so that their living together couldn't be a negative mark with NASA.

They moved to Houston and we kept in touch. I got married. Bill was eventually accepted into astronaut training a few years later. I was envious and somewhat taken aback by their success. I was finishing up residency, and had accepted a position on the faculty at UCLA Harbor, but then my husband got a job in Milwaukee at Marquette University, and we moved there.

I was restless and wanted only to apply to NASA. I kept in touch with Bill and Anna, who regaled me with tales of their experiences in astronaut training. When I finally submitted my application in the next selection cycle, Bill informed me that I was definitely one of the finalists they were considering; but then the results came in, and I had not been selected. Bill suggested that it was because I was a psychiatrist. He'd been there long enough to realize that psychological issues were not highly esteemed in the universe of flying and engineering. He and Anna recommended that I apply for a position as a flight surgeon in the Flight Medicine Office which supported the astronauts. A position had just opened and NASA was looking for a woman who could take care of the new women selected as astronauts. However, I was warned that I should keep my psychiatry experience to myself, or de-emphasize it on my application. So I did. While waiting to apply to be an astronaut, I had tried to beef up my resume. I had taken flying lessons; obtained a master's degree in biochemistry and the equivalent of one in bioengineering. I was in good physical shape.

Lo and behold, NASA hired me as one of several flight surgeons in the Flight Medicine Office. The three of us laughed about it, because I then became Bill's and Anna's physician, as well as physician to all the other astronauts in the Shuttle Program. Flight Medicine was also responsible for supporting the Shuttle space missions and had a position in Mission Control to monitor health issues.

I was so excited! My dreams were coming true. The person I was replacing in Flight Medicine at the Johnson Space Center had just been selected as an astronaut herself, and so I thought the chances were good that eventually they would see my abilities and potential, and then I, too, would be selected. Just be patient, I told myself.

My husband was none too thrilled, and I look back now and see that his anger at my decision to go to Houston did not bode well for the long-term success of our marriage. I didn't care. I moved to Houston and left him in Milwaukee. In my arrogance, I thought I was leaving him and the marriage behind, and it didn't matter to me at the time if he followed me or not. That's the kind of person I was.

Like medical school, NASA was not what I imagined it to be. I had thought of the agency as a state-of-the-art scientific and engineering marvel, and NASA took great pains to project that image. But the truth was that they were at least a decade behind "state-of-the-art" in any area. Yes, they could boast of having the "best and brightest," but they also had the absolute worst. It took me some time to realize that NASA was actually just a typical federal government agency—the post office in space, so to speak—and that, like all such agencies, they were run by those who valued power over others more than anything else. Mediocrity abounded. The quest for power was what it was all about, and that generated a pettiness and ruthlessness that was astonishing, even for someone like me whose idealism had already been jaded years before.

No matter. I set to work to make my mark on the agency. The actual space missions were exciting beyond my wildest dreams. When I worked in Mission Control either during a simulation or during a real flight, it was like being on the bridge of the *Starship Enterprise* with the Flight Director in the role of Captain Kirk and "lil' ole me" as Bones McCoy sitting at the surgeon console. I would

My official NASA photo.

Here, I am working at the Surgeon's Console during a space mission.

have been content, I think, just supporting the missions even if I didn't become an actual astronaut. My first mission as Surgeon in Mission Control was, appropriately enough, to support Bill's first assigned mission in space. It was an incredible experience that I would not trade for anything. I had written a highly-regarded lead article for the *Journal of American Psychiatry*, probably the most prestigious journal in the field, and it was titled "The Journey Out and In: Psychiatry and Space Exploration." I had made my mark, I felt. I had successfully combined the two big conflicting areas of my life: the inward introspective study of the mind, and the outward exploration of the universe. I was happier than I had ever been.

One of the great aspects of being at NASA was all the travel to strange and interesting places that related to the job. One of my most vivid memories was going to the old Soviet Union with a Congressional delegation to celebrate the anniversary of the Apollo-Soyuz mission. This was the trip that made me once and for all understand the psychological and spiritual devastation (along with the material poverty) that accompanies communism and socialism (and all totalitarian ideologies). The Russian people were friendly, but many of them were without hope or joy. I was surprised that almost everyone I met in the sciences drank to excess. The researchers and scientists I met were desperate to present their work to other scientists outside the Soviet Union, because they did not get to travel outside the country, and the Soviet journals censored their writings and interspersed their results with phrases like, "Glory to Soviet science!" We actually saw banners with that propaganda hanging from the exterior walls of the Institute of Biomedical Sciences where we spent much of our time. During the day and in public, the people we met were stern, and vocal apologists for the communist regime. At night, in their homes they were completely different people who spoke openly to us (albeit in whispers) of their unhappiness and lack of belief in the future. One night, I was with two young men, one of whom was an interpreter and the other supposedly a scientist. Both secretly confessed to me at dinner, while greatly intoxicated, that they were actually KGB informers sent to "get information" from me about the recent military space flight for which I had been assigned as crew surgeon. "Don't tell us anything important," they insisted kindly. Instead, we got very drunk and ended up in Red Square on a snowy evening, where I taught them to dance to the Wizard of Oz song *Ding Dong, The Witch is Dead.*

We danced on the red bricks of the square up to St. Basil's Cathedral, which used to be a house of worship but had been taken over by the Communists. One of my new friends started to cry as he told me that his grandfather used to tell him stories about the saints and remembered going to the Cathedral to worship when he was young. "We don't believe in anything anymore," he said sadly.

Challenger

On January 28, 1986, I was at Cape Canaveral in Florida. As a NASA Flight Surgeon, I had been assigned as the Crew Surgeon for Mission 51-L, better known as *Challenger*. The other flight surgeons did not want the job since there were many in the Agency who disapproved of having a civilian—the teacher in space—fly on a space mission. The crew had trained together for over a year, and I had come to know them all very well in the course of the training and medical preparation. I had been at the Cape for over a week and the launch had been scrubbed several times for a variety of reasons. I was staying in a cheap motel in Cocoa Beach as we waited for weather to permit the launch attempt.

One of the memories I have of that time is a CBS evening news broadcast with Dan Rather on January 27th, who questioned whether NASA would ever be able to launch a space mission on time. He then proceeded to go down a long list of shuttle missions that had been delayed. I remember being annoyed at the time because of the unspoken expectation by Mr. Rather that launching a complex space vehicle like the shuttle was a simple thing, and it was inexplicable that there should be problems or glitches.

We had scrubbed the launch several times at the last minute, but everyone was fairly certain that we would get a "go for launch" on January 28th, since President Reagan's State of the Union address was scheduled for that evening, and he intended to mention the teacher-in-space, Christa McAuliffe. The Agency would not want to disappoint the President.

When I woke up the morning of the 28th, it took me only a few minutes to apprehend that the launch would again likely be postponed. It was 19 degrees outside! This was unusually cold for Cocoa Beach, even in January, and, used to the warm weather year round in Florida, I had not even brought a sweater with me. In the

In addition to working in mission control, I was sent to the Air Force for flight surgeon training and training in piloting a T-37 "Tweetie Bird" jet aircraft.

The crew of Space Shuttle mission STS-51-L pose for their official portrait on November 15, 1985. In the back row from left to right: Ellison S. Onizuka, Sharon Christa McAuliffe, Greg Jarvis, and Judy Resnik. In the front row from left to right: Michael J. Smith, Dick Scobee, and Ron McNair. Source: NASA.

15+ minute drive to Launch Control, I continually shivered from the cold, because there was no heat in the car I had rented either. I wore just a cotton pantsuit with my flight jacket.

In Launch Control, there was a great deal of buzz about the temperature. From the console I monitored there, I listened with interest to the discussion. The countdown was proceeding, but there had been ice spotted on the external tank, and crews were sent to check it out. All of us there fully expected another launch scrub. I was at the Surgeon's Console, which monitored crew health, and directed emergency medical operations in the case of a catastrophic event on the launch pad, or for an RTLS abort (return to launch site). We joked and talked among ourselves, commenting on the crew status. The Surgeon Console was one of the few which were able to listen to crew chitchat in the shuttle prior to launch.

Much to all of our surprise, after a delay, the countdown was resumed. It had been decided that it was safe to proceed. I remember that we were surprised because no shuttle had launched in such cold weather before, but we all assumed that this had been thoroughly discussed at a higher level. We were privy only to the comments that were in the LCC (Launch Control Center in Florida). The Management Team had met outside the LCC.

The countdown proceeded, and *Challenger* was launched. As soon as it lifted off the pad, control of the mission was transferred to the MCC (Mission Control Center in Houston). It was at this point that most of the LCC team could relax and turn around to watch the shuttle ascend. There were large windows in the roof which gave us a prime view of the entire ascent, from about three miles away. I watched with my usual sense of wonderment that humans had been able to manipulate so much energy and use it to escape the planet.

My awe was short-lived as an anomaly appeared in the instruments. Something seemed to have gone wrong with the SRBs (solid rocket boosters), and they detached from the ET (external tank) too soon after launch. There seemed to be a big explosion, but none of us was certain what might have happened. I swung into action, because it seemed that we must be in an RTLS situation. I made a few commands to my emergency team, who were outside in ambulances, as I continued to watch the growing cloud of the explosion, waiting for the orbiter to appear from behind it, heading back to the emergency landing site, not far away.

I waited and waited. The *Challenger* did not emerge from the explosion. I felt a momentary confusion, and then I think all the blood must have drained out of my head as I comprehended what this must mean. The crew must have been killed. All of them. I had to hold onto the console for support. All I could think was, *Oh my God, oh my God.*

The Launch Director coolly called for a lockdown. No one was to leave the room until all information on all consoles was safely secured. It was then that I was able to gather myself together again, as I recognized that if the crew was gone, my responsibility was to take care of their families. I went to the Launch Director and asked to be allowed to leave, because the families were in Crew Quarters, about a mile or so down the road. After some discussion, the doors were unlocked and I was permitted out. I ran to my car and started down the road, but everyone on the highway had stopped to watch the launch and the road was blocked in both directions. People were milling around, still not accepting what they had just seen with their own eyes.

I was desperate to get to the families and do something useful. I wasn't sure what, but I felt they might need me there. I drove my car on the center divider and the grass between the lanes, and made my way through the crowds who had stopped to watch the launch. It took me some 20 minutes to get to Crew Quarters.

The next twelve hours are something of a blur. I had read about mass hysteria in textbooks, but that term is far too mild for what I found when I reached the place the crew called home prior to a launch. All the members of the immediate and extended families were there. Women were screaming, babies were crying. People thronged around me, wanting to know if the crew had parachuted to safety. I was stunned that they had not yet grasped what had happened. One family member was certain that a rescue plane would find the crew in the ocean somewhere. Several people fainted. I needed help to medically manage the 30 or more family members who were there, but George Abbey, the head of Flight Crew Ops, would not permit me to call in any other doctor. Finally, however, he permitted one of the nursing staff at the Cape to assist me. He was in full damage control mode, and wouldn't permit any TVs or radios to be turned on, either. Certainly, no phone calls. One family member required hospitalization, due to disorientation and confusion. Abbey said no, he wouldn't let me do that. I replied that I was the doctor, not him, and did it anyway. That decision, it turns out, effectively ended any chance of my being selected as an astronaut.

Abbey forbade anyone to leave the Cape and head back to Houston (where everyone lived and where their entire social support was), until after Vice President Bush arrived. The Vice President was an emissary sent by President Reagan to console the families. Bush landed at KSC about 8:00 pm that night, and by then I was exhausted and could barely stand up. I barely remember being introduced to Mr. Bush and shaking his hand. The closest I came to crying was when I heard the wife of the Shuttle Commander (Dick Scobee) say in a quavering voice to Bush that her husband would not want space exploration to be halted or NASA punished in any way because of what had happened that day. Beneath the grieving was an underlying fear that we all shared at the time that this tragedy would have negative political consequences for NASA, which despite its image, was basically a political government program and therefore subject to the whims of politicians. Its scientific mission was second to this reality.

After Bush left, most of the families were hustled onto NASA planes to go back to Houston. I had to remain, however, because the person I had hospitalized at the nearby Air Force hospital would not be able to fly back until the next day, and I was to accompany that family. But reinforcements had arrived as other astronauts had flown to the Cape, so I gratefully collapsed into a bed at Crew Quarters.

I flew home the next day with my patient and the family. On the afternoon of the 29th, I finally made it home where my husband—who was waiting for me—handed me about 100 phone messages from just about everyone I knew. When he took me in his arms, I finally started to cry and didn't stop for several hours.

For the next five years, I was unable to talk about what had happened that day without becoming completely choked up and unable to speak. I still get tears in my eyes as I remember the event and the memorial service a few days later, where I had the honor of meeting President Ronald Reagan and Nancy.

It was an extremely emotional and sad day. President Reagan arrived to honor the fallen crew and to heal the nation at a large ceremony for which the entire Johnson Space Center was present, along with assorted federal and local dignitaries.

As the crew surgeon for that mission, I accompanied the families of the crew to a private meeting with the President before he spoke to the large crowd of employees and officials. I felt a little out of place at this private meeting, so I tried to stay off to the side as, one by one, Reagan greeted all the immediate family members and talked with them.

Much to my surprise, after he had visited with them for a while, the President walked over to where I was standing. Apparently he had asked who I was, because he addressed me as "Doctor" and held out his hand, saying, "It must be especially hard for you today to have lost those who looked up to you as their doctor and who put their trust in you." He said it very quietly, and his sincerity and genuine concern for what I was experiencing brought tears to my eyes. Until that moment, I had managed to keep it all together and not show my feelings in public.

The next thing I knew, the President of the United States had put his hand on my shoulder and was comforting me, telling me that he understood my loss and that he knew I had been trying to be strong and take care of all the family members of the crew, but that he could see I was suffering, too.

I had voted for Reagan in both the '79 and '84 elections (it was the first time I had voted Republican instead of Libertarian), but it wasn't until that moment that I truly understood the personal power of the man, his genuine warmth and the depth of his concern for someone he didn't even know. He instinctively seemed to understand that I had deliberately put aside my personal feelings about the tragedy because I had the awesome responsibility of taking care of all the crew family members (who were also my patients).

It crossed my mind even then, that he was telling me how much he identified with my situation and the responsibilities of my job. He had an entire nation to take care of, but he still personally mourned for those who had died. It could be that I read too much into what he said, but I don't think so. He could have ignored me since I was standing off to the side from all the family members. But he went out of his way to find out who I was and then chose to come over to talk to me.

I remember telling him in a choked voice how much his understanding meant to me, and he looked at me with those clear, direct eyes of his and said, "You will be able to handle it. I know you will."

It seemed to me that I stared into those eyes for a long time (but it was probably only seconds), and then he turned away and signaled to the others that it was time to start the memorial service.

I actually got to stand on the platform while he spoke. This had been the spot prearranged for me to be so I would be able to observe the families in the front row and be ready to respond if they needed me. I couldn't have been more than ten feet or so away from the President during his remarks.

I never spoke to President Reagan again, but at the end of the ceremony, after the missing man formation of T-38's had flown overhead, I accidently caught his eye, and he winked at me.

Needless to say, I will always remember his kindness and strength.

I can't remember if I said a prayer during all this grieving, personal and professional. Many of the family members were devout Christians, and I noticed that those people seemed to cope much better with their mourning.

NASA as an organization coped with the *Challenger* disaster very poorly. The Agency used a combination of denial and intellectualization/rationalization to avoid dealing directly with the mindset and culture that had ignored safety and avoided dealing with uncomfortable technical and psychological issues. In the months that followed, I finally faced the reality that the Agency I had idealized for so long was actually corrupt and primarily concerned with covering its own mistakes—just as any political organization would do. They were caught up in *hubris* and groupthink; they had believed in their own "sunshine and lollipops" press for too long. Instead of making changes in the culture that had led to this catastrophe, they were only concerned with making sure everyone *thought* they had made the changes. The appearance was more important than the reality.

I had been a general flight surgeon before, and now, for the first time, I began to look at NASA with a psychiatrist's eyes. And what I saw disturbed me greatly—especially the way they handled the fact that the crew had NOT died immediately in the explosion as we had all believed when witnessing the explosion, but had been alive, but likely unconscious, until the crew compartment crashed into the ocean. I watched as they tried to hide this truth from the public and from the families. I also watched as they carried out the external motions of changing the culture, but from the inside I witnessed no change in attitude or behavior.

It has been quite a number of years since that cold morning when *Challenger* and her crew were lost. In 2003 when *Columbia* disintegrated on reentry, killing all the crew onboard, many of my old friends called me because I had predicted that NASA would have another preventable tragedy. I would like to think that we learned something from the space missions we have lost—Apollo 1, *Challenger*, and *Columbia*—but I really don't know whether NASA has learned anything. Even more now than when I was there, the Agency is a political football. I refer you to Jim Oberg, an MSNBC space analyst and close friend, who has this to say today about all three disasters:

> Spaceflight has its own inherent hazards, and if not respected, any of many factors can kill people. Recognizing this, engineers install backup hardware and escape systems and build in allowances for uncertainties—all in an attempt to keep such external hazards at bay.
>
> The debris from the disasters remained safely hidden away, comfortably out of sight and—as experience would show—tragically out of mind.
>
> But the internal hazards—what investigation boards have called the "flawed safety culture"—have proven much more insidious. This is the realm of convenient assumptions, of complacency, of willfulness, of use of statistical superstitions, of a false familiarity with an unblinking foe. It is a culture made possible by an all-too-human aversion to facing unpleasantness.
>
> It has become easy to look away from these horrible space disasters—and I never call them "accidents," a term that relieves the people involved on the ground of ultimate responsibility.

NASA prefers to literally bury the wreckage in underground concrete crypts, to shove the investigation reports onto another bookshelf, and to allocate one day per year to honoring the dead while ignoring what killed them the other 364 days.[16]

Sigh…. That's human nature for you. That day especially, but all my years at NASA, taught me a very important lesson about reality: *Reality does not care about your feelings.* It exists outside of you and what you think and feel.

Obviously I'm not the first person to discover this fundamental truth. Many people believe that this means that only science can be the source of truth, and therefore of reality. But it took a great national disaster like this one to get me thinking again about exactly what truth is and exactly how we go about understanding reality. Reality says that if a frozen O-ring cracks, then fuel will leak and possibly lead to a catastrophic explosion. But it also says that love, compassion and caring exist and make a difference in peoples' lives. Is that difference simply a matter of the movement of unseen chemical particles? Is space the only "final frontier"? Or, is there another frontier that goes beyond the physical particles and mechanistic interactions that make up the universe and truly give meaning to human life? Our perception of reality must take into account the non-physical, non-mechanical realities that permeate our lives: the encounters we have with others that change us; the tragedies that occur with which we must cope; the hopes and disappointments we have about our lives that can lead us to become better people—or not. Could I admit to myself that there was a spiritual dimension to our collective life here on this planet? Now I was getting into the realm of poetry and art.

My dreams of space exploration, the journey out, were a means of escape from a world of pain, misery and evil. But this disappointing world also had within it the possibility of compassion and love between people, and I still believed in the triumph of good over evil. But to think about these things requires a journey *inward*: to understand who we are, where we come from and why we are here. Both the journey in and out can lead to darkness. My favorite poet, T.S.

---

16 Oberg, James. Deadly Space Lessons Go Unheeded. MSNBC Commentary. 1/26/2005. http://www.nbcnews.comd/6872105/ns/technology_and_science-space/t/deadly-space-lessons-go-unheeded/#.XOhQ5Zh_NPZ

Eliot, wrote about the desire to escape from "the darkness outside and within":

> *Why should men love the Church?*
> *Why should they love her laws?*
> *She tells them of Life and Death,*
> *and of all that they would forget.*
> *She is tender where they would be hard,*
> *and hard where they like to be soft.*
> *She tells them of Evil and Sin,*
> *and other unpleasant facts.*
> *They constantly try to escape*
> *From the darkness outside and within*
> *By dreaming of systems so perfect*
> *that no one will need to be good.*
> *But the man that is will shadow*
> *The man that pretends to be.[17]*

The darkness and lifelessness of space surrounds the beauty and life of our planet. Space, though it was to be my escape, inadvertently pointed me to contemplating the heavens. And I could not think of the cosmos without experiencing that sense of wonder and awe at the idea of mankind exploring the vast universe.

Reflecting the Light of the Son

The moon generates no light of its own, but is bright in the sky because it reflects the light of the sun. This is symbolic of how Catholics think of Mary, whose role is to reflect and participate in the shining glory of God.

Similarly, as the moon is, in our own day, increasingly viewed as a "launching pad" for reaching more distant outposts in space, so Our Lady is the "white ladder" that joins heaven and earth. Ultimately, the meaning of all space endeavors is tied to the acknowledgment of God, the Creator of the whole universe. Here, too, the beauty of the heavens is a sign of the most beautiful creature ever made—the Mother of God—who herself leads us to the All-Beautiful One.

Before Jesus, the Son of God, came into the world, the pagans considered the heavens, that is, the sky and the stars, to be the

---

17 Eliot, T.S. Choruses from *The Rock,* Verse VI.

abode of the gods. In the Old Testament, man is invited to reflect upon the beauty of the starry heavens and, from there, raise his mind to contemplate the God who created them. We can, thus, draw an analogy between space travel and that spiritual journey toward God—a spiritual journey beginning in this world and ending in heaven to dwell with him forever.

The moon is a well-known and ancient symbol of Mary, the Mother of God. Just as the moon reflects the light of the sun, so the splendor of the Immaculate Virgin Mary reflects the light of the true Sun, God himself. And because Mary brought this light, Jesus Christ, who is God, to us, she can help us in developing a relationship with God. In the case of space travel, the moon is being viewed as a middle ground or base acting in an "intercessory" fashion, i.e., to help "bring" more distant posts "closer" to us, just as Mary brings God close to us. So, the rocket scientists may be closer to our spiritual Mother than they think.

Going from Earth to space using rockets and using the moon as a waypoint is like going from worldly material concerns to union with God, with the help of Mary as our spiritual Mother and Mediatrix. Both journeys start by recognizing the limitations of where we are at and crossing the threshold of new frontiers: astronauts opening new colonies on planets and space stations; people of faith reaching out in prayer beyond this material, created world to God and, ultimately, to heaven. The moon provides the help for the difficult journey to Mars and beyond. Mary helps in the journey to God, bringing us to her divine Son.

If the moon is for the glory of mankind, then Mary is for the glory of God. Materialism excludes the spiritual realities, and this exclusivity explains its divisiveness, drawing people into small exclusive groups, boxing them in and setting them against each other. Materialism is the spiritual equivalent of being stuck on a planet without a rocket. In contrast, supernatural faith transcends material limitations, reaching out to the infinite God. It is the ultimate in "thinking outside of the box." By its nature it is unitive, because it has for its object God who is one, the eternal unchanging source of all real unity. It breaks the self-indulgent, self-centered aspect of materialism. Our longing to go to the stars, therefore, is akin to a longing for heaven and God, even if not everyone is ready to acknowledge that longing deep within their hearts which have been created for fulfillment in God.

Acknowledgement and authentic development of the spiritual dimension is what is needed to place our technological endeavors in their proper perspective, such that they can truly be harnessed to reap the hoped-for fruits of unity, peace and true progress. Mary is the focal point, because her Son is both God and Man, divine and human natures united in one divine Person. He brings God and mankind together, and this union took place in the womb of Mary. Devotion to Mary keeps the human family united together, because they will then be united to and in God. We come to an encounter with God through the motherly solicitude of Mary.[18]

A Great Sign Appeared in the Heavens

Then God's temple in heaven was opened, and the ark of his covenant could be seen in the temple. There were flashes of lightning, rumblings, and peals of thunder, an earthquake, and a violent hailstorm.

A great sign appeared in the sky, a woman—clothed with the sun, with the moon under her feet, and on her head a crown of twelve stars. She was with child and wailed aloud in pain as she labored to give birth. Then another sign appeared in the sky; it was a huge red dragon, with seven heads and ten horns, and on its heads were seven diadems. Its tail swept away a third of the stars in the sky and hurled them down to the earth. Then the dragon stood before the woman about to give birth, to devour her child when she gave birth. She gave birth to a son, a male child, destined to rule all the nations with an iron rod. Her child was caught up to God and his throne. (Revelation 11:19–12:2)

This image of the Woman from Revelation is symbolic of many things (including Israel and the Church), but Catholics also recognize her as the Mother of God.

Psalm 19 tells us, "The heavens declare the glory of God; the firmament proclaims the works of his hands." One of the greatest creations of God was Mary, born without original sin, perfect in her union with the will of God, and it is in the heavens that Mary is proclaimed.

In September 2017, it came to my attention that Revelation 12 was revealed in an arrangement of celestial bodies that was a tableau of the Gospel:

---

18 Burk, Roderic. "Mary to the Moon! *Mission Immaculatae*. Vol. 14, No. 4, July/Aug 2018. https://missiomagazine.com/mary=to=the-moon/

On that date, the sun was in the zodiac constellation Virgo—"*a woman clothed with the sun.*" The moon was at the feet of Virgo—"*with the moon under her feet.*" The "nine" stars of the zodiac constellation Leo, plus three planets (Mercury, Venus, and Mars), were at the head of Virgo—"*on her head a crown of 12 stars.*" The planet Jupiter was in the center of Virgo, and would pass through the constellation—"*She was with child and wailed aloud in pain as she labored to give birth.*" Jupiter is the largest of the planets, the "king" of the planets, so to speak—"*She gave birth to a son, a male child, destined to rule all the nations with an iron rod.*"[19]

As I read this explanation at *The Catholic Astronomer*, it caused me to remember my obsession with the stars and my time at NASA. My greatest defense against the troubles in this world was to get into a rocket ship and fly away. But, wherever you go, there He is. You can't escape from yourself, let alone the Creator of the Universe. He pursues you relentlessly, and even sends His Mother after you so you won't be frightened. Like the two directions in the circle of the rosary, both lead to the center, where Truth and God reside. Mary guided me in both directions, since both journeys inevitably led to her Son.

She helped me to understand what my real calling in life was all along. She was there when I witnessed the healing power of my fourth year resident, James. She was there in the personal interaction that led to me deciding to go into psychiatry and the study of the mind. She was always there, though I didn't realize it until much later, steering me back towards her Son, back to the truth of Him and the truth of myself. How could I have thought that I could escape Him forever? He planned my life long ago, and everything that happened, for good or for ill, happened for His purpose and ultimately for my good. I was a lost sheep, a prodigal daughter, wandering around, barely able to survive spiritually; and He sent His Blessed Mother to rescue me and bring me back. He "knit me together in my mother's womb," and now He was knitting the pieces of my life together again through my spiritual mother. From the beginning as a child, there was an invisible cord that bound me to Him, and in all my wanderings, though it stretched to the breaking point, it never

19 Graney, C. "Biblical Signs in the Sky? *The Catholic Astronomer*/Sacred Space Astronomy. Sept. 23, 2017. https://www.vofoundation.org/blog/biblical-signs-sky-september-23-2017/

broke and it never became untethered. The thread was tied in Baptism and strengthened in Confirmation. I suspect that another layer of understanding the meaning of Mary's rosary is the appreciation of it as a spiritual rope that connects those who pray it to God. I was foolish enough to think that this lovely sacramental was just a means of meditation, when it is not only a powerful weapon, but also a strong rope that held onto me all those years away and then pulled me back home.

Oh, Mary, Queen of the Heavens and Earth, how gently you tugged on that rope so that even I did not realize how lovingly I was being drawn back into your motherly arms and into His Story. Let me be born again through you, tender Mother.

Salve Regina

Salve, Regina, Mater misericordiæ,
vita, dulcedo, et spes nostra, salve.
Ad te clamamus exsules filii Hevæ,
Ad te suspiramus, gementes et flentes
in hac lacrimarum valle.
Eia, ergo, advocata nostra, illos tuos
misericordes oculos ad nos converte;
Et Jesum, benedictum fructum ventris tui,
nobis post hoc exsilium ostende.
O clemens, O pia, O dulcis Virgo Maria.

Ora pro nobis, sancta Dei Genitrix.
Ut digni efficiamur promissionibus Christi.

CHAPTER 6

I WILL NOT LEAVE YOU ORPHANED

Poor Sylvia

Death so young
Does not become a woman.
She never knew
A father's love,
Like most of us she grew
Without it.
She never cried
For Mommy's kiss,
Instead she dreamed
Of love's sweet bliss.

Some can stand
The isolation
Doing well
With guilt and
Without love.
Others for their
Own reasons,
Though dad and mommy's dead
And gone before they're grown,
Cannot forget.
They turn themselves
Inside out,
Raging at the world
In poems.

Orphaned

My mother died in 1998 from liver failure. She was 72 years old. In her last months, she suffered intermittently from hepatic encephalopathy and was at times confused, disoriented and emotionally labile. She had been living with my brother Paul for some months, and Paul and his wife Pam had tried to take care of her, but one thing they would not do was to allow her to drink.

Alcohol was what had brought her to the state she was in. We didn't realize that she was an alcoholic until it had progressed far along in its path of destruction. From what we were able to figure out, she probably started drinking excessively after she and Glen broke up, but she was sly about it, having one or two scotches during her dinner and keeping a bottle or two at home for the lonely evenings. She had always been prone to ill temper, especially when she didn't get her way, and the alcohol magnified this characteristic to the extreme.

She hated living at my brother's home because she could not drink. She would say, "Everyone has to die someday, and this is the way I choose to die." Eventually, she got so angry that one day, she just left and found an apartment down the road where she could drink to her heart's content.

I don't suppose I will ever understand the loneliness and desperation she must have felt most of her life that drove her to be so persistently self-destructive. I remember one heart-to-heart conversation we had a few years before the end. I had made relative peace with her, accepting that she would never understand me either. I never told her about Glen's abuse of me or talked to her about it, but I think she knew and was sorry but just couldn't say it to me. She was aware that I wanted nothing to do with Glen and although he and she eventually divorced and he had remarried, she decided to have an extramarital affair with him anyway. This lasted all the way up till the time of her death.

A few years before her death, I received word that I was going to get an Alumni Award from UC Riverside and was invited to the awards dinner in Riverside where Mom still lived. I flew out and invited her to the dinner with me. Without my knowledge, she invited Glen to accompany us. I was very angry when I found out,

My mother, Anne Ceglia Santy Cannell.

but she pleaded with me that since he was one of the Deans at the University giving me the award, that everything would be all right. That was also when she confessed that she was seeing him behind his wife's back. She felt it was poetic justice. I swallowed my anger at his being present and decided to go along with the whole charade. At dinner that night, Glen was unbearable. He made allusions to how I had grown up into a decent looking young woman. "You know, I always thought of you and your brothers as white trash, but you proved me wrong about that," he laughed as he sipped his wine. I was furious and, standing up I tossed my glass of wine in his face and walked out of the hall.

Later that evening, my mother called me at the hotel I was staying at. I think she had somehow imagined that Glen and I would "make up" and that was why she had arranged for him to accompany us. Or, perhaps she felt that my getting this prestigious award from the University would change his mind about her children being "white trash." He certainly made no secret of his attitude when they were married, and I had felt some sympathy for her then, thinking it must hurt her feelings. I didn't realize that her drinking problem began shortly after their divorce and continued even when she thought she had "won him back" from the other woman. Except for drinking to cope with her anguish over the path her life had taken, my mother and I had many similar personality characteristics (much as I hate to admit it). I had some of her good qualities also, though, including her intelligence and determination.

She never brought up the subject of Glen again, but I knew that she was still seeing him regularly, behind the back of his current wife. She once told me, "I like being the 'other' woman instead of the wife who is cheated on."

One evening not that long after the incident with Glen, she had a few drinks at dinner and confessed to me, "You know, my mother never loved me. She loved Pauline (her sister) more than she could ever love me. Pauline was always the perfect one as far as she was concerned." This confession was unexpected and I thought it was an opportune moment to bring up my own grievances regarding her mothering. She started to cry when I did. "My father really, really disliked me too, and always wished I had been a son. So they ignored me until my brother Paul came along." She looked wistful. "They loved Pauline and Paul, but they hated poor Antoinette." The scotch she was drinking made her morose. "I tried to be a good mother to you, I really did. I always promised myself that I would not act the way my mother acted toward me, and you're saying I did exactly the same thing." She was inconsolable and eventually I just took her home. I felt remorse that I had even brought up the subject. What made me think that this was a topic we could ever really discuss or come to grips with? We never mentioned her parents or our relationship again, but I resolved not to upset her further and to try to make things better for her.

It was shortly after that painful interaction that she asked me to come to the doctor's office with her, "because I can't understand what he's telling me." The doctor had just informed her that she had end stage liver disease. I had noticed that her skin was turning a bit yellowish, but she told me she was "just getting a tan." The doctor minced no words in explaining his diagnosis again when I was present. He told her she had about a year to live unless she completely stopped drinking. There was nothing that could be done to reverse the process going on in her liver, but if she stopped drinking, then she might live two or three more years—at most. Either way, she was going to die from the booze.

Mom tried to brazen it out by insisting she wanted a second opinion. "Get as many opinions as you like," he told her bluntly. When she came out of the doctor's office with me, she asked me what she should do. I told her she needed to stop drinking and suggested that she might move in with Paul and Pam. "Don't you think he was exaggerating a bit?" she asked me. "I'm not really dying, am I?" I thought to myself that this was the kind of psychological denial she had exhibited for most of her life. Why was I in any way surprised that she would use this defense now? For the first time, I admitted to myself that my mother met almost all the psychiatric criteria for Narcissistic Personality Disorder (I avoided the thought that I shared some of the same narcissistic traits).

She moved to Fresno to live with my brother a few weeks later after constant pressure from Paul, Pam and me that she stop drinking and that this would be impossible if she continued to live alone. She only lasted a few short months under my brother's supervision.

After she moved out of Paul's home and into an apartment, we assume the drinking began again. In a last-ditch effort to get her to stop, I asked her where she wanted to travel to in the whole world and I would take her there. To my surprise, she told me Nashville and the Grand Ole Opry Hotel. She was a country music fan and had always dreamed of going there. So, I arranged a Christmas visit when the hotel was lit up like nothing you've ever seen before. I also took along my six-year-old daughter and the three of us had a magical trip on that 4-day vacation to Nashville.

Mom and I spent a lot of the time talking. She admitted that she could not give up drinking. She told me that she knew I thought she was going to die, but she was going to see some specialists and was optimistic that she wasn't. She was gay and cheerful until I caught her paying one of the bellboys to bring her a bottle of scotch to our room on the sly so I wouldn't find out. Then she became piteous, crying and accusing me of hating her and trying to make her suffer.

The end came not long after our trip. I returned to Michigan where Norm, Alexandra and I were living, and a few weeks later got a call from my brother begging me to come out and "get some help for Mom." She had started acting confused and disoriented and would not let my brother take her to a doctor or emergency room. I flew out right away and was able to convince her to go back to the ER with me. Pam told me that just before I arrived they had dragged her to the ER in spite of her protestations and that when a young, handsome doctor walked into the room, my mother, sitting pathetically in a wheel chair looking bedraggled and unkempt, magically transformed herself, sitting up straight, smiling and playfully interacting with the young physician as he examined her. "Pat, it was unbelievable," Pam told me. "One minute she seemed to be at death's door, the next she was animated and flirting with the doctor." Needless to say, the doctor told Paul and Pam that he didn't see that she needed hospitalization or any particular emergency treatment. But when I moved in to stay with her for a while, it was clear that she could not take care of herself. I had to bathe and dress her because she was too weak and too confused to do it herself. I found dozens of empty scotch whiskey bottles under the sink. Finally, I convinced her that she needed to at least "dry out" in the hospital where it would be safe, and we got her admitted for some care and alcohol detox. That night, after we went back home and left her in her room at the hospital, she became confused and agitated, screaming and pulling out her IV, not understanding where she was or why she was there. The on-call doctor gave an order for some parenteral Valium, not realizing that mom was in hepatic failure; and because Valium is metabolized by the liver, the medication was more than her damaged system could handle. She promptly went into what is called "hepatic coma."

The next morning when we came to see her, we found her in a vegetative and unresponsive state. For the next few days we took turns staying at her bedside, hoping she would wake up. The doctors were grave and told us that her waking up was very unlikely and that this was the "end stage" of her liver disease. On the third day of our vigil, my sister-in-law and I came back from lunch and as we walked into the room, my comatose mother suddenly sat up in bed and, looking straight at me, said very clearly, "I love you." I burst into tears and ran over to hug her, but she was already slipping back into the coma. "You said I wouldn't feel any pain," she whispered. "Patty, I'm suffering. Please help me." I promised her I would and then she was unresponsive again. This kind of sudden and brief awakening happens a lot with dying persons and even with those who are comatose. Something within makes them muster all the strength they have left to say goodbye to their loved ones, despite death's imminent arrival.

Determined to fulfill her last wish, I marched up to the nurse's station and demanded to talk to the doctor. I told him that I knew they had made an error by giving someone in hepatic failure a drug and if they didn't want me to sue them, they could make sure that she wasn't suffering. The doctor suggested a morphine drip. As a physician, I knew what that meant: the rate of the morphine drip would slowly be increased until respiratory arrest occurred, then death. They knew and I knew that this was the end. "She won't suffer," the doctor reassured me. "Morphine causes pleasant dreams." I agreed, knowing that I was signing her death warrant. I didn't tell my brother about the morphine, but I insisted on spending that night in the room with Mom. I also insisted that a priest be called to give her the last rites.

In retrospect, I marvel that at this critical moment one of the first things I thought of was my mother's eternal soul. Had I started believing in God? I guess I wanted to hedge my bets with regard to my mother, who had been told by her priest some years before that she could no longer receive Communion because of her divorce and because she had confessed to adultery and did not plan on stopping her behavior. My mother had announced to me at the time, "The Catholic Church can go to hell as far as I'm concerned."

Nevertheless, I insisted that a priest be called, and the hospital arranged for a Franciscan monk from a nearby monastery to come to give her the Rite. In spite of both of us having consigned the Catholic Church to hades in our separate ways, I believe it was by the grace of God that she was able to get the sacraments before her death.

The priest was a short balding man, dressed in a brown robe and wearing sandals, the perfect image of a monk. He performed the last rites that are given to the dying, and even recited the special prayer for pardon of sins, while I stood there watching. When he was done, he told me not to worry. My mother would go "straight to heaven" because her sins had been forgiven. "Doesn't it matter that she is in a coma and can't actually repent?" I asked, perhaps a bit sarcastically. "No. It doesn't matter. She's been baptized and confirmed. She will be all right. God has mercy in situations like this. Thank you for asking me to come." Surprisingly, I felt at peace about her impending death and thought that Mom would be pleased.

I can't fully explain how comforting the priest's words were, though my suspicious and somewhat judgmental mind wondered if heaven was indeed a possibility for her. In that moment, I think, I transitioned from being a hard-core atheist to being an ambivalent agnostic, admitting that maybe there was a possibility that God existed. I know that I truly hoped my mother would get into heaven and finally be happy.

But my spiritual awakening was not yet completed. The nurses agreeably brought in a cot for me to sleep on when I told them I would spend the night. I fell asleep near her, and I had the strangest dream. In the dream, I was chasing a beautiful white horse which teased me by letting me catch up to it, but then would quickly run away from me. Suddenly the horse broke into a gallop and I could see that it was headed for a cliff. I shouted for the horse to stop, but it only increased its headlong rush and, when it reached the cliff it leaped off in a magnificent exhibit of strength and beauty. Horrified and then astonished, I watched as the beautiful creature turned into a winged Pegasus, and, instead of falling, spread those lovely wings and flew off into the clouds. I woke up then and immediately went to my mother's side. I heard her take a few agonizing breaths; then the breathing stopped. There was no pulse. I pushed the call light and waited for the nurse to come, while I quietly cried. Then I called my brother and told him that mom was gone.

My father passed away a few years later. He died quietly, alone, from a heart attack in the night. My brother had moved into a large house that happened to have a little cottage in back and he invited my father to live there. It was the perfect arrangement since my father's health was declining from his diabetes and heart disease. Sadly, he only lived there for a few months before his death.

I flew out to California for the funeral. I felt the same kind of regret for his death that I had felt for my mother's. So little had been said between us that really mattered! With my father, the only topics of conversation were either the Yankees or the Marines, the only two things he ever really cared about.

I know that in their own way, both of my parents loved my brothers and me to the best of their capabilities. They were not bad people. Still, there was something broken in each of them that prevented them from being able to convey that love. Neither of them was very religious, and neither of them ever talked about God that I can remember. They passed through their lives without ever thinking about the "Big Questions of Existence" that seemed to consume me all the time. Or, if they did have thoughts about life, the universe and everything, they never communicated that to anyone that I was aware. I'm sure they both had regrets about their life, but again, those regrets did not seem to cause them to change behaviors or alter their lives in any way. I think of them often and pray frequently for their souls. Perhaps the Lord, in His infinite mercy, has judged them gently. I do what I can from this side of eternity.

May the souls of the dear departed, through the mercy of God, rest in peace. Amen.

My father, Frank Santy.

The Atheist's Substitute for Faith

Recognizing and accepting my mother's and my narcissism was actually very empowering in an unexpected way. I found that I had a knack for dealing with narcissistic and borderline patients in my psychiatric practice and began to specialize in their treatment. Understanding my own pathology made it easier to empathize with these individuals, who often had tales of abuse and neglect when they were young that would make any listener think he or she had grown up in the fields of heaven by contrast. Because I could understand them, I didn't make most of the mistakes that other therapists make in dealing with these patients' painful past. In particular, I did not "walk on eggshells" in trying to deflect their anger and resentment but tried to honestly and directly help them to confront the complicated issues and conflicts that animated their destructive behaviors.

For years pop psychology and its gurus have attempted to counter the despair created by modernism's toxic culture by proposing many self-help guides whose tenets have slowly percolated through K-12 educational curricula and been accepted wholeheartedly by the cultural elite of Hollywood, the intellectual elite of academia and by those in the political arena.

The triumvirate of contradictions that claim to be based on "scientific" psychology includes the hyping of (1) self-esteem (increasing your self-worth without having to achieve anything); (2) hope (achieving your goals without any real effort) and (3) victimhood (it's not your fault that you haven't achieved anything or made any effort).

These three fundamental axioms of current cultural thought have risen in acceptance even as the concept of *personal responsibility* has been denigrated and mocked. Even the use of the *words* has become politically incorrect—racist, even—primarily because personal responsibility is not compatible with the way modern society presents and encourages all forms of perceived oppression and victimhood. Being a victim has, in itself, become the most powerful weapon that can be used against others to obtain power and revenge in modern society.

Michael Novak, U.S. ambassador and the George Frederick Jewett Scholar in Religion, Philosophy, and Public Policy at the American Enterprise Institute from 1983 until 2009, has noted, "Modernity tore down the only philosophical foundations which can sustain a free society." He went on to say in a speech at Westminster Abbey after receiving the Templeton Prize in 1994:

> The 20th century was not only the bloodiest but also the most ideological. Ideology is the atheists' substitute for faith. Lacking faith, lacking God, the 20th century was a continuous battle of ideologies.[20]

Except for politics and economics, nowhere is this conflict more manifest than in my own field of psychiatry and psychology, where the human consequences of the dominant ideologies promoting narcissism, sociopathy, and nihilism, are damaged and broken families (both parents and children).

After several decades, the intellectual impoverishment brought about by faux self-esteem, fairy-tale utopian fantasies, and eternal victimhood—all pseudoscientific psychological deceptions designed to maintain dependence on the ideology and simultaneously accumulate power—have become apparent to anyone who has eyes to see. In "Self-Help's Big Lie," Steve Salerno writes:

> Over a 20-year span beginning in the early 1970s, the average SAT score fell by 35 points. But in that same period, the contingent of college-bound seniors who boasted an A or B average jumped from 28% to an astonishing 83%, as teachers felt increasing pressure to adopt more "supportive" grading policies. Tellingly, in a 1989 study of comparative math skills among students in eight nations, Americans ranked lowest in overall competence, Koreans highest—but when researchers asked the students how good they thought they were at math, the results were exactly opposite: Americans highest, Koreans lowest. Meanwhile, data from 1999's omnibus Third International Mathematics and Science Study, ranking 12th-graders from 23 nations, put U.S. students in 20th place, besting only South Africa, Lithuania and Cyprus.
>
> Still, the U.S. keeps dressing its young in their emperors' new egos, passing them on to the next set of empowering curricula. If

---

20 Novak, Michael. "Awakening from Nihilism." Templeton Prize Address, August, 1994. https://www.firstthings.com/article/1994/08/awakening-from-nihilismthe-templeton-prize-address

you teach at the college level, as I do, at some point you will be confronted with a student seeking redress over the grade you gave him because "I'm pre-med!" Not until such students reach med school do they encounter truly inelastic standards: a comeuppance for them but a reprieve for those who otherwise might find ourselves anesthetized beneath their second-rate scalpel.

The larger point is that society has embraced such concepts as self-esteem and confidence despite scant evidence that they facilitate positive outcomes. The work of psychologists Roy Baumeister and Martin Seligman suggests that often, high self-worth is actually a marker for negative behavior, as found in sociopaths and drug kingpins.[21]

We see the people who have deeply imbibed this "psychology-lite" poison everywhere around us and in all levels of society. Particularly we can notice it in the elites of Hollywood, academia and politics, who alternate between acting out their narcissistically-fueled superiority—demanding to be noticed, admired and loved (by you), and playing the narcissistically-empowered victim—demanding their inalienable rights and privileges (at your expense).

But the real victims of all this hype are children, because these foolish notions, without a scintilla of scientific evidence and only because it makes some people feel good about themselves, have become the pop psychology dogma of public policy in education; and the corollary of their implementation is an equal and opposite *de-emphasis on taking personal responsibility for one's actions and behaviors and accepting the consequences, both good and bad.* One's character is not only determined by successes in life, but also by how failures are dealt with. Self-esteem is the by-product of negotiating those successes and failures with integrity and honesty. "Hope" is meaningless unless it escapes the land of fantasy and conforms to reality; and victimhood, while real in some cases, should only be a transient state that motivates a person to change behavior—not a celebration or a way of life.

While most of the emphasis in talking about narcissism is an emphasis on the "selfish" aspects, there is a flip side to "selfish" narcissism—and that is *narcissism rooted in idealism* rather than in selfishness, also known as "idealistic" narcissism. This second

---

21 Salerno, Steve. "Self-Help's Big Lie," *Los Angeles Times*, January 1, 2006.

kind of narcissism (the flip side of the coin, if you will) is less obvious to an observer, since it is disguised with a veneer of concern for others. But it is equally—if not more—destructive and causative of human suffering, societal decay, death and misery. The idealistic narcissist is invested in utopian fantasies, while the selfish narcissist engages in personal grandiosity. The former's self-esteem is derived from the power they feel in controlling the lives of others, and they desperately need to maintain a constant supply of "victims" they can pretend to champion. In general, they are extremely resistant to taking responsibility for their own behavior or the implementation of their utopian dreams—all of which have been emotionally catastrophic for the individuals in the system. Grandiose and selfish narcissists are preoccupied with their personal delusions of perfection and superiority, and they end up destroying relationships and making life miserable for themselves and others around them. *Personal responsibility* becomes a dangerous and radical concept that threatens their view of themselves and their world view. In a world where personal responsibility and accountability for one's behavior is expected, they themselves would have to answer to that thing we call "reality." Both types of narcissist must constantly engage in psychological denial in order to maintain their façade of superiority.

Hence an entire system has been constructed (called "political correctness") to stigmatize and intimidate those who believe that self-esteem must be earned by achievement and is dependent on one's choices and actions; that "hope and change" come about not by wishing and lovely rhetoric, but by *doing*; and that your current bad situation may not be (entirely) your own fault, but by constantly externalizing blame for that situation, you miss opportunities to make necessary changes in your own behavior that keep you down. By taking responsibility for your own life, you stop waiting to be rescued and do what you have to do to rescue yourself. You can stay a "victim" and wallow in "victimhood," but the essence of maturity and adulthood is taking charge of your own life and not letting others dictate who you should be or what you should do. Freedom is not "just another word for nothin' left to lose," but having the option to choose what is right and good.

Unhealthy narcissism of either type is encouraged by the "self-esteem gurus" in education, whose nonsense continues to reinforce the inappropriate grandiosity of young children by facilitating a faux self-esteem, just as the politically correct, "kum-bay-yah" types (among other groups) continue to reinforce the *malignant selflessness* that comes from fervently believing in the perfectibility of human beings and the establishment of heaven on earth.

Between these two influences unleashed on the vulnerable minds of our children, is it any surprise that by the time they get to college, kids are either dysfunctional, self-absorbed narcissists, naively malignant do-gooders, or (at best) completely and irrevocably cynical about the pervasive indoctrination and anti-intellectualism they have been subjected to in their educational careers and well on their way to dismissing the existence of God and embracing a nihilistic world view where there is nothing left to lose? Those of us who come from broken homes are particularly vulnerable.

This digression into narcissism shows how much time I subsequently spent thinking about the topic after the death of my mother. Somehow, it seemed to me, this was the key to understanding the pathology that infected my family and then myself, and which led me to believe that I was the center of the universe and all that mattered was my own happiness and pleasure, and that everything was about ME and my needs. At the same time, this subjective philosophy allows a person to actively impose virtue on others and then feel good about one's own pure motives. After my mother's death, I was only just beginning to understand the basic etiology of a world view that required the abandonment of God and then worshipping personal pleasure and controlling others. This world view leads inevitably to broken individuals and broken relationships. It fractured my parents' marriage—and was destroying my own life, with my full consent.

Much as I hated to admit it, I had become my mother. How was it possible that the trauma that had destroyed my family and scarred my own life was now being acted out again in my generation by myself? How could I so easily succumb to the lure of pursuing pleasure and self-gratification at the expense of those I supposedly loved? This disastrous freedom that I had embraced in the women's movement was only hyped, unreal self-esteem, wrapped in a mantle of faux victimhood. It justified all my rationalizations for abortion, adultery, fornication and every other evil in which I indulged myself.

And, though it took me somewhat aback to think it, the problem of my generation was not physical; nor was it psychological or emotional, but primarily spiritual. We were living in an era that was gleefully proclaiming that God was dead and anything goes.

My mother, father and stepfather were completely immersed in their feelings and obsessed with themselves. In the end, they didn't care whom they hurt as long as they satisfied their own desires. This is a harsh judgment, perhaps, but I make it knowing full well that I was in no way different from them. The once hopeful individualism of the Enlightenment has morphed during our age into a philosophy that solely emphasizes one's own will and one's own feelings, to the exclusion of reason, reality and God. Is it any wonder that this can create monsters who destroy families, cultures, and even nations?

Behold Your Mother

Michael Novak stated further in "Awakening to Nihilism":

The grand refusal of the modern age to say "yes" to God is a failure both of intellect and of imagination. Modernity's mistake is to have imagined God as if He were different from truth, alien to ourselves, "out there" like a ghostly object far in space to serve Whom is to lose our own autonomy. Modernity has imagined God to be a ghostly version of the tyrants we have actually seen in the 20th century.

It took the real tyrants of our time, jackbooted, oily-haired, self-confident, enjoying the torture of innocents, to shatter that false identity. The tyrants may have thought they were like God; it was idiotic to flatter them that God was like them.[22]

It is Mary of Nazareth who can teach us the humility that is needed to say "yes" to God. In her response to the Angel at the Annunciation, she was able to say, "Behold the handmaid of the Lord. Be it done to me according to thy word." (Luke 1:38) The entire universe awaited the Virgin's *fiat* so that it could become whole again.

And later in Luke, Jesus, dying on the Cross, says to all of us throughout the generations of man, "Behold your Mother." This was very deliberate, as was everything that Jesus did during His life.

22 Novack, ibid.

He is near death and in agonizing pain, and one of His last acts is to entrust us to His Mother and her to us. Even in agony, He was thinking only of our well-being.

In my wildest imaginings, I could never be the loving and self-sacrificing mother that Mary was to Jesus, or exhibit the boundless love He must have felt for her—especially while I was so busy acting out against God and licking my own wounds, raging at the world in poems while at the same time trying to "save it" from oppression and tyranny for which I myself was partly responsible.

No, Jesus did not leave us orphaned. Not only did He send the Holy Spirit on Pentecost to the Disciples in the upper room (including His Mother, who was there with them); He also gifted His Blessed Mother to the Beloved Disciple when He was on the Cross. "From that day, he took her to live with him," John's Gospel relates. And since that day we too have had the choice of taking her in to live with us.

Aren't we all who are in the Body of Christ His "beloved disciples"? Mary became our spiritual mother on that day, and we need to take her in to live with us as John did.

Father Michael Gaitley, MIC writes regarding St. Louis de Montfort's devotion to Mary:

> At Baptism, we're transformed into members of the Body of Christ, made into "other Christs."
>
> Baptism also has to do with the Holy Spirit. I say this because it was the Holy Spirit who first formed Christ, and it is the Holy Spirit who continues to form other Christs—the members of Christ's Body—at every Baptism.
>
> Now, who does the Holy Spirit use to form Christ: He uses Mary, even though he has no absolute need of her. So for example, he made use of Mary at the Annunciation, which led to the birth of Jesus Christ our Savior. He made use of Mary just before Pentecost, which led to the birth of the Body of Christ, the Church. He makes use of Mary at every Baptism, which gives birth to "other Christs," the members of his Body. The Holy Spirit always makes use of Mary to give birth to Christ![23]

---

23 Gaitley, Michael. 2013. *33 Days to Morning Glory.* Marian Press. Stockbridge, MA. Pp 108-9.

I'm sorry that I never got a chance to talk to my own mother about faith. It was one of many topics on which we never conversed. I wish I were able to discuss it with her now that I am no longer an atheist or even an agnostic, but a believer.

Certainly in my own life, I have come to appreciate the power of grace and how it works. I believe that God never completely abandons us, but retreats from the picture to a position of watchful waiting. When He sees even the slightest movement toward Truth, He sheds a tiny ray of His grace on us through His handmaid, Mary, His beloved daughter, mother and spouse—a ray of grace which enhances and rewards that turn to Truth. Once grace has entered, it prepares the way for even more grace to pour in until suddenly, without the person even realizing it, they are standing before Truth Himself.

It happens gradually, then all at once. Thus, a lifetime of denial can end in the most sudden of conversions, where one is at one moment a denier or doubter and, in the next, overshadowed by the Spirit and reborn into a whole new paradigm of existence, reality and truth.

Born again, from the Mother of Truth!

Memorare

Remember, O most gracious Virgin Mary, that never was it known that anyone who fled to thy protection, implored thy help, or sought thine intercession was left unaided.
Inspired by this confidence, I fly unto thee, O Virgin of virgins, my mother; to thee do I come, before thee I stand, sinful and sorrowful. O Mother of the Word Incarnate, despise not my petitions, but in thy mercy hear and answer me. Amen.

CHAPTER 7

DEAR DOCTOR

Dear Doctor

You come to me wounded,
On sweaty summer nights
The pain is raw and therapy divine.
How can I heal you?
How can I cry?
Your blood stains my hands,
Your eyes my mind.
Am I your Savior, or
Do you pray to other gods before me?

Suffering is your burden, you are mine;
I will die more horribly than you,
Piece by screaming piece.
What do you say?
"I know if I could be saved,
You would save me"?
Dear God! What can I do?
You come to me, wounded;
Can I come to you?

Praying to Other Gods

When I first decided to go into psychiatry, I was certain that this was the medical field that managed to combine all the different areas I was interested in or passionate about. Unlike surgery, there was a strong interpersonal aspect to it and, as I had found out in medical school, I was not only good at what they call "interpersonal sensitivity," but I also felt personally comforted in some way by my interaction with patients. I truly felt that by this personal connection I was doing them some good; and likewise, they were doing something for me. It seemed like a fair exchange.

As I mentioned earlier, my classmates were disappointed in my choice of specialties. After all, I had told everyone that I planned to be a surgeon and, up until my experiences in my third and fourth year clerkships in surgery, that plan held firm.

One of my favorite quotes about psychiatry is from Harry Stack Sullivan whose work I greatly admired: "An enthusiasm about psychiatry is preposterous—it shows one just hasn't grown up; but at the same time, for the psychiatrist to be indifferent toward his work is fatal." My enthusiasm about psychiatry was very adolescent and idealistic; and above all my vacillation between surgery and psychiatry demonstrated to me that I was still rebelling against God, but at the same time wanted to be proved wrong about His existence. How, you might ask? I think my desire to become a surgeon was in essence a desire to have power over life and death. Of all medical specialties, surgery is the one where the physician is of necessity most god-like, impersonal and detached. Don't think that I am judging surgeons negatively, however. Their difficult jobs call for an excess of clinical detachment in order for both them and their patients to survive. And, at the other end of the scale was psychiatry, where relationships and caring were of the utmost importance: *"for the psychiatrist to be indifferent toward his work is fatal."* I clearly see that the attraction to psychiatry for me was the connections that it facilitated between doctor and patient. Those connections were essential for the patient's healing; and, I might add, were essential for my own healing. God is in the relationship. In fact, God *is* relationship. He is a relationship of love between three persons: Father, Son, and Holy Spirit. Yet He is One Being and One Nature.

As a surgeon, I could be fully elevated to the god-like status that many surgeons aspire to and are shown by others; but as a psychiatrist, the lowliest of the medical specialties (at least it was when I chose it) I could still keep my connection to human frailty and deal with something more important than organs and disease.

These two extremes of thinking dominated most of my life and so it is to be expected that they would dominate my attitude in my chosen profession. I could still not decide between the splintered pieces of the piano...or, the music that came from it.

Back in the day when I entered this specialty, psychiatry was controlled by psychoanalysts; and psychodynamic theories like Freud's or Jung's prevailed over more physiologic theories. Learning about Freud and the great theorists of the mind was very exciting and as I delved into concepts like the "unconscious," transference and counter-transference, and the like, I found myself increasingly fascinated by these ideas, which sought to describe certain areas of life that could not be measured or materially grasped. On the other hand, I was convinced that the field was on the cusp of exciting biological discoveries about consciousness and thought; and this dovetailed with my atheistic orientation and wanting to reduce human thought, behavior and even existence into purely materialistic chemical interactions.

I never forgot my biochemistry training and became adept at psychopharmacology and combining medication and psychotherapy in my treatment of mental illnesses. For a while I toyed with the idea of joining a psychoanalytic school, but the closest I came to entering was to decide on psychoanalytic therapy for myself. The first analyst that I saw ended up in disaster. He was a handsome 45+ year old gentleman who was very kind and sympathetic, but after a few months, when I really started opening up about very intimate issues, like my unhappy sex life, instead of steering me through the mess I was making of my life and understanding all the disastrous relationships I had entered since leaving home and having the abortion, he seduced me. I know that sounds passive, but it wasn't really. I admit to being a willing partner to the seduction and for a while, it was terribly exciting. He was wealthy and happened to own the beach house that Spencer Tracy and Katherine Hepburn had their affair in, and I can't tell you how awesome it was to think of myself as some sort of modern-day Hepburn. He asked me to call him Rhett (after Rhett Butler in *Gone with the Wind*). He was married with grown children and considerably older than I was.

I came to my senses after several months and realized how utterly stupid it was to be having an affair with him. He was a big deal in the Psychoanalytic Institute and he was becoming increasingly paranoid about the affair becoming public. This is what caused me to realize that he wasn't all that concerned about me at all. Stepping back psychologically from the relationship, I could see what a big mistake he had made in initiating this affair with me; but I also could see what a bigger mistake I had made in letting it happen. Rhett was concerned for his social status in the community; I became increasingly concerned about my emotional status. In today's bizarre culture, this story is a perfect *#metoo* moment, or would be if it hadn't been a profound learning experience for me about making bad choices. No one forced me to have sex with my therapist.

Here I was, an unhappy medical student and soon-to-be psychiatric resident trying to resolve some of the emotional and spiritual scars I had already picked up in my short life. He knew about my stepfather's inappropriateness with me and how it had impacted me, yet that did not deter him. To be honest, it didn't initially deter me, but I couldn't help but wonder after a while if I wasn't reliving that episode in my life and hoping it would turn out better. Freud called this the "repetition compulsion." Things turned out basically the same. I left home because of my stepfather; I left therapy because of my therapist. Except, I wasn't a teenager anymore.

When I broke it off with him, I was astonished that he expected me to continue in my therapy sessions with him anyway. I told him I would find another analyst. He became frightened and in my rush to reassure him, I promised that I would never tell anyone about our affair. When he heard that I had made an appointment with Kato Van Leeuwen, another well-known psychoanalyst in the area, he was devastated because she and her husband socialized with him and his wife. Again I vowed not to reveal what had happened and told him he was just going to have to trust me.

He didn't need to worry. I kept my word—more because I was ashamed of the whole affair, rather than any personal integrity on my part. I ruthlessly castigated myself about what a stupid mistake I had made. I was worse off psychologically than before I went to see him and in despair because I was becoming more and more like my mother: desperate for the attention of men.

Therapy with Kato went very well. I kept my vow over the next seven years, although I did refer to the relationship with Rhett in a circumspect way. Seven years! I went twice and sometimes three times a week for seven years! The therapy cost about 75% of my income as an intern and resident, so during that time I lived in abject poverty in a total dump of an apartment in Santa Monica. But in the end, I suspect it was one of the best investments I could have made in myself.

I came to slowly understand my self-destructive side, and to understand my guilt and sadness over my parents' divorce. As I slowly explored my feelings towards my parents, I could see how the craziness of my family had tormented me and made me unhappy. I also began to understand why psychiatry had been suddenly so attractive to me. I wrote earlier about my intense desire to escape the confines of our planet and journey into outer space. What I didn't realize was that by taking care of the emotional problems of others, I was trying to undo my own emotional traumas.

A major event in my life occurred while I was in this analytic therapy. My best friend from medical school committed suicide. Sigrid was everything I wanted to be: beautiful, perfect and exceptionally graceful and intelligent. All men, everywhere were instantly attracted to her. She could go to the supermarket and by the time she finished getting her groceries, she would have had several men hit on her. Yet, she was horribly insecure. She married a Ken-doll kind of person (who saw her as his complement Barbie). He was a few years ahead of us in medical school and they seemed happy for a while, but then the marriage broke apart when he could not contain his jealousy. Sigrid started dating a series of men, but every relationship ended because she would break it off. They would all then come to me, begging me to intercede for them. One particular boyfriend was her senior resident in obstetrics. I had met him several times and felt some attraction to him myself. When she broke up with him, he asked me out on a date. To be sure that he was no longer seeing Sigrid, I contacted her and asked her if she was truly done with the relationship because otherwise I would never consider dating him.

Sigrid assured me that she was perfectly ok with him and me dating. I remember we talked about any number of things and compared our residency experiences. She was at Cedars-Sinai doing an OB/GYN residency, while I was at Harbor/UCLA in my internship year. We even made plans to meet for dinner the next week. That same night, she took an overdose of barbiturates and was found dead the next day by her neighbor.

I was distraught and couldn't believe she had killed herself. I had gone out that night with her ex-boyfriend after she had told me it was no big deal, and now she was dead. I blamed myself for not appreciating what she must have been feeling, and I could hardly function. When I had been called (she had listed me as next of kin) I was working on the medical ward at the medical center and I was so upset I pulled the phone out of the wall and threw it into the Nurses' Station. It didn't help that Sigrid's mother also blamed me, angrily screaming at me that she had Sigrid's diary and that Sigrid had hated me and been envious of me! This did not compute at all. My analyst was stunned also because Sigrid had contacted her in the weeks before her suicide and was thinking of starting therapy with her. I had not known this, but it provided a link between us that the therapy further enhanced. It took me a long time to get over the feeling that somehow I was to blame for her death. I told her all the secrets of my heart and my life, but had no idea that she was not truly reciprocating. Once again, I had failed to make a connection with someone who was important to me.

I think of Sigrid sometimes and what a waste her death was. But she was not the only casualty of residency. Two other classmates of mine committed suicide that year and several of my patients, which demonstrates not only how stressful internship and residency were then, but also how fragile and vulnerable we humans are. Most people don't appreciate that while psychiatry doesn't deal directly with death, there is death all around, and I felt surrounded by it.

Although my life was a mess and therapy was both difficult and painful, it seemed to help bring some order into my life.

I finally terminated my sessions with Kato a week before my marriage. I felt that I had finally come to understand myself and that I was "cured" of my neurotic tendencies. Isn't it amazing how people can lie so glibly to themselves? Of course, my relationship with Norman seemed fairly healthy for a while, but the same old conflicts eventually arose, as you have seen. I had the same hole in my heart that had never been filled, not even by marriage, and I suspect never would have been filled by any man. What was it St. Augustine said?

"Thou hast made us for thyself, O Lord, and our heart is restless until it finds its rest in thee."

Yes, that essentially sums it up. After seven years of therapy and twenty-seven years of marriage, I came to the realization that I was still not happy, and that the source of my unhappiness lay in the relationship with my mother and my father. Yes, my earthly mother and father and their conflicts and poor choices had impacted me greatly, but the true emptiness of my life was in not knowing or accepting the love that was right there within my grasp from my spiritual Father and Mother. I had never truly healed that hole in my heart and never would as long as I thought it could be filled in this life.

I think that in the field of psychiatry, my relationships with patients were probably as stabilizing for me (maybe more so) as they were for them. And, if psychiatry had stayed the same as it was when I entered it, I might have eventually worked through some of the emotional pain I still carried around with me.

But, the psychiatric field didn't remain static. It changed, and not for the better, I think. Psychiatrists like myself were in increasingly short supply, and soon it became less and less acceptable for a physician/psychiatrist to do psychotherapy, the part of psychiatry that I loved the most, as insurance companies refused to pay for such therapy except with lesser-trained and less expensive alternatives. When I was in my analytic therapy, I paid for every cent of it out of my own pocket. I never expected medical insurance (which was very basic in those days) to pay for it. But soon, everyone started expecting that insurance should pay for psychotherapy and, since insurance companies wouldn't compensate for psychotherapy with an M.D. psychiatrist, people started to see other mental health professionals. That's how psychiatrists became relegated to only prescribing medications. Doctors were supposed to prescribe medications was the rationale; and they get highly paid for doing so. I hated focusing only on the biological. Even if I had wanted to spend time on the psychological or even the spiritual aspects of a patient's problems, I was only scheduled a mere twenty-thirty minutes a month with most patients.

My years in psychiatry probably made me a better person. It was during my time spent with really ill patients that I truly began to care about others in a way that finally took my focus off myself and my own little concerns. I learned so much from them all; it was they who taught me true empathy. Compared to most of them, my own life had been a breeze, it seemed. One of my earliest patients was a 15-year-old young woman, Angie, who had been abused for years by her father and whose mother had been completely oblivious to the abuse. Angie withdrew into fantasy and imagined herself in a universe where she was ferociously protected by gigantic alien cats who destroyed anyone who threatened her and also took her on exciting space adventures. She was a talented artist and painted these adventures, and her paintings captivated me. At times she would lapse for weeks into a profound psychosis and require hospitalization. She was actively suicidal when I first met her and only marginally responsive to medication. My clinical supervisor, a dedicated research psychiatrist, told me that if I agreed to do psychotherapy with her, I was taking her on for life. I started therapy with her and took his words to heart. Although Angie and I are no longer officially doctor/patient, we are still in regular contact some 45 years later. She never committed suicide, and she has made a positive life for herself, despite her chronic mental illness. I stopped seeing her when I moved to Wisconsin after my marriage, but we talked many times over the years since then, and I have come to love her as a daughter. She lives in a small Northern California town where she is celebrated as an artist in the mental health community. I have several of her paintings hanging in my house.

Dear God, What Can I Do?

I had many patients over the years, and what I learned from them was that something important was missing from medicine and psychiatry. That "something" became even more obvious as I watched psychiatry abandon psychotherapy and embrace a purely biological approach to the problem of human suffering. We were all just bunches of chemicals and clumps of cells now.

Absent was an effort to address the spiritual emptiness from which most of our patients suffer—an emptiness bordering on nihilism and leading to ever-increasing drug and alcohol abuse and suicide. This is an emptiness that cannot be filled with pills of any sort, which only add to the problem in a vicious cycle of problem→ drugs → worse problems→ more drugs until all hope is gone and happiness completely out of reach.

Don't misunderstand me: there are real psychiatric illnesses and diseases, but the vast majority of people suffer from the effects of being human and living in a less-than-perfect world. I was often witness to the evil that men (and women) can do to each other. It tore me apart inside.

Like my first experience as a medical student with the dying surgical patient Mary, sometimes all I could do was to listen and care in a world that does neither. Very often patients would not even be in the least "compliant" (meaning they did not do what we prescribed or what they needed to do to get better or improve their lives). They would not consider ceasing the use of drugs or alcohol (like my mother); they would choose to remain in situations where they were abused and mistreated; and, if they did try to alter things, they would frequently end up in the same situation all over again in a short time. Some people would call that a "disease," but I think it is only human nature in a disordered world.

It reminded me of the lines from Macbeth:

Macbeth: How does your patient, doctor?

Doctor: Not so sick, my lord, as she is troubled with thick-coming fancies that keep her from rest.

Macbeth: Cure her of that! Canst thou not minister to a mind diseased, pluck from the memory a rooted sorrow, raze out the written troubles of the brain, and with some sweet oblivious antidote cleanse the stuffed bosom of that perilous stuff which weighs upon her heart?

How comforting it would be to "cure her of that!" If only we could do what Macbeth suggests. But those "rooted sorrows" and "written troubles" can't be erased with drugs except when those drugs render unconsciousness. Many have been formulated to bring "sweet oblivion," and the result is the opioid epidemic and a consequent meteoric rise in suicide. Embracing unconsciousness is no way to live your life, but I can understand the spiritual emptiness that leads a person to try.

What makes life worthwhile? What makes life meaningful? These are the questions that our entire culture is trying to avoid asking or answering by escaping into the oblivion promised by drugs, the bliss promised by mindless sex and hook-ups, and delight in the materialistic accumulation of "things." Such are the dead ends of a culture that has left God behind in its pursuit of pleasure, abandonment of reason and glorification of the self.

It doesn't take a rocket scientist—or an avowed atheist/agnostic—to realize that something is fundamentally wrong and getting worse.

Mary: A Counter to Hopelessness

Living a Christian life in an aggressively secular and hostile world is not easy, and it becomes less easy by the day as our postmodern world eagerly chips away at even the semblance of virtue. Regrettably, I didn't even try to live such a life for more than fifty years. I turned away from God completely and fully embraced the toxicity of the anti-Mary, the poison of narcissism and the "culture of death" that encourages abortion, euthanasia, and all manner of "compassionate" murder and hate. The evils infecting our times have damaged so many souls; and these souls cannot be made whole by the mere application of psychiatric therapies and chemical formulas.

Pope Emeritus Benedict XVI writes:

The power of evil arises from our refusal to love God....

A world without God can only be a world without meaning. For where, then, does everything that is come from? In any case, it has no spiritual purpose. It is somehow simply there and has neither any goal nor any sense. Then there are no standards of good or evil. Then only what is stronger than the other can assert itself. Power is then the only principle. Truth does not count. It actually does not exist. Only if things have a spiritual reason, are intended and conceived—only if there is a Creator God who is good and wants the good—can the life of man also have meaning. [24]

Most of the people who came to me in my psychiatric practice were souls without spiritual purpose—souls who were desperately

---

24 Benedict XVI. "The Church and the Scandal of Sexual Abuse." Catholic News Agency, April 10, 2019. https://www.catholicnewsagency.com/news/full text-of-benedict-xvi-the-church-and-the-scandal-of-sexual-abuse.59639

seeking something and discovering that all the societal promises of free love, free sex, free drugs, self-fulfillment, "do whatever you feel" were hollow assurances that led to nothing. They could not understand why they were so miserable and believed that a "pill" could fix their lives and make everything better. They failed to recognize the source of their misery and were reluctant to change anything about themselves or their lives. Instead, they would stubbornly cling to the false promises which were so seductive. Like me, they wanted love, yet somehow love always remained elusive. They wanted happiness and were miserable; freedom, and yet they remained in chains. All of us were lost souls. I would dutifully prescribe a pill (though usually not the one they wanted) and hope for the best. I would refer them to therapy also, but many refused to go or said they couldn't take the time, or there were no therapists available to see them. Soon psychiatry became a job I was beginning to hate because all the relationship had gone out of it. Patients were only interested in the pill and that was all I had to give them.

But there is a counter to the vast hopelessness that I was mired in personally and professionally. There is a Way. Christ promised that it would not be easy, but it would lead to inner peace and happiness, no matter what was happening in the world.

First, virtue, the old bugaboo that even the pagan philosopher Aristotle believed was absolutely necessary for a civil and good society, must be reclaimed. Virtue is an old-fashioned concept. Living virtuously and consciously practicing the seven virtues (faith, hope, charity, prudence, temperance, justice and fortitude) is considered foolish in our jaded times: "*Now the natural person* does not accept what pertains to the Spirit of God, for to him it is foolishness, and he cannot understand it, because it is judged spiritually...." (1 Corinthians 2:14).

The perfect example of those virtues lived in life is Mary. Women especially need Mary, the epitome of true femininity, as we try to negotiate a joyful path through the varying demands of marriage, motherhood, parenting, and career. In good times and bad times, Mary retained a quiet peace and true freedom that only comes from an absolute commitment to the will of God. Sometimes I permit myself to feel the regret of not having perceived this truth for so long. How many of my own troubles in all the spheres of my life might have been handled with the grace and serenity that Mary radiated her entire life? How much time I wasted in willfully withholding my love from my God and refusing His faithful love in my life! I thought I could have it all: love, marriage and career; but I couldn't keep any of it until I controlled my own will and began to listen to what God was trying to say to me. The contemplation of the life and sorrows of the Blessed Virgin opened my eyes and my ears. And although I am still a novice in virtue, with the grace of God to sustain me, I will get better in practicing virtue in my everyday life, even within a culture somewhat hostile to such virtues.

The Ten Evangelical Virtues of the Blessed Virgin Mary are actually recorded in the Gospels. She is considered:

1. Most Pure (Mt 1:18, 20, 23; Lk 1:27, 34);

2. Most Prudent (Lk 2:19, 51)

3. Most Humble (Lk 1:48)

4. Most Faithful (Lk 1:45; Jn 2:5)

5. Most Devout (Lk 1:46-7; Acts 1:14)

6. Most Obedient (Lk 1:38; 2:21-2, 27)

7. Most Poor (Lk 2:7)

8. Most Patient (Jn 19:25)

9. Most Merciful (Lk 1:39, 56)

10. Most Sorrowful (Lk 2:35)

Although she does not speak many words in Sacred Scripture, the words and actions in which Our Blessed Mother engages are filled with meaning and purpose and give us a foundation upon which to build our own virtue. In the Bible, Mary pondered many things in her heart. She thought carefully about what God's will was in every situation and kept herself open to His Word in her life. At the Annunciation she gave her *fiat* to becoming the mother of mankind's Savior. In the Temple after finding the young Jesus, she gave expression to a common lament of parents everywhere and discovered that there is a higher authority that must be obeyed beyond honoring one's parents. At Cana, she said, "Do whatever he tells you" and expressed the wisdom of one who both loves and trusts as she leads everyone to her Holy Son, the second person of the Trinity.

Mary's virtues, listed above, demonstrate a total and selfless commitment to doing whatever is God's will—no matter what suffering must be endured. And, in spite of any suffering, she shows us that one can be filled with patience and humility that comes from love and devotion to God. Rich or poor, we are all called to practice these virtues—that is, if we want to find a "peace that passes all understanding." That is what is missing from the lives of so many these days—both those who seek psychiatric help, and those who are just trying to get through life. Their souls—and my soul—simply cannot find rest until they rest in the One who is Lord and Creator of us all. Leaving out the spiritual dimension in our lives is like leaving out the most essential ingredient of a recipe and expecting the final product to be palatable. It will taste like sawdust.

The Magnificat

My soul proclaims the greatness of the Lord,
My spirit rejoices in God my savior,
For He has looked with favor on His lowly servant.
From this day all generations will call me blessed:
The Almighty has done great things for me,
and holy is His Name.
He has mercy on those who fear Him in every generation.
He has shown the strength of His arm,
He has scattered the proud in their conceit.
He has cast down the mighty from their thrones
and has lifted up the lowly.
He has filled the hungry with good things,
and the rich He has sent away empty.
He has come to the help of His servant Israel,
for He has remembered His promise of mercy,
The promise He made to our fathers,
to Abraham and His children forever.
Glory to the Father, and to the Son, and to the Holy Spirit,
as it was in the beginning, is now, and will be forever. Amen.

CHAPTER 8

REDEMPTION

In the Shadow of a Cross

Whispers of ancient litanies
Weave through gleaming rosaries,
While Mass is said in distant rooms,
And voices echo from empty tombs.

In darkness, prayer-candles paganly dance
On altars of indifference, where chance
Offers a communion of death and fear
To all the people praying there.

And saints who pray for peace on earth,
Are answered by a godless mirth;
The devil and unholy fathers,
Wonder why the world bothers?

But He who died for all man's sins,
Already knows the side that wins.

The Side That Wins

I already revealed in the first chapter how my somewhat one-sided disagreement with God was ultimately resolved. And if you continued reading after that, you may have observed that I behaved like a petulant child for most of my life, sulking because I didn't get my wishes granted and making bad choices in my life because I thought I knew better than God. This contrariness and willfulness was my way of thumbing my nose at Him. If the ways of God were the same as man's, then all of us poor humans would get what we want, when we want it, all the time—and woe to us! We humans on our little piece of earth think we are so smart, but how can we possibly see the big picture that includes millions of humans (some behaving like me), or even all the nearly infinite number of molecules in the universe? Or even how all of that relates to every other individual person, let alone every molecule in the universe?

Lest we forget (and I did), God made us from nothing and holds each one of us and all the universe in existence from moment to moment. If He turned His attention away, even for a brief span of time, we would all cease to exist. Poof! Think about that for a while.

Frank Sheed comments:

> If God, having made us, left us, we should be kept in existence by the material used in our making—namely nothing.

> This is the truth about the universe as a whole and every part of it (including ourselves). Unless from moment to moment God held it in being, it would simply cease...

> What it is made of does not account for any being's coming into existence or remaining in existence; everything depends at every instant upon the God it is made by. That is one reason for giving the whole power of our mind to knowing God.[25]

Pondering this fundamental reality, I can now appreciate that God must love the human race (and me!) unconditionally and wants only what is good for us (and me!). But under this reality is another sobering truth: if God wants the best for each one of us, then every single one of our choices, every action that we take in our life, has a ripple effect on the lives of those around us throughout all of time!

---

25 Sheed, Frank. (1957) *Theology for Beginners.* Aeterna Press, New York. p. 39

This is known in chaos theory as the "butterfly effect" and the theory holds that a minute, localized change in a complex system can have large effects elsewhere. If that is the case, then only an omnipotent and omniscient God can work to bring about the best possible outcome in a world of people given free will. This is how His plan of salvation works. By freely cooperating with Him, we help ourselves and others. By actively working against His will, we hurt ourselves and others. Only an infinitely merciful God who truly cares for His creation could hold all of this together and juggle the pieces of everyone's puzzle so that everything fits together perfectly.

When bad things happen, there is always—always—an unseen and unknowable (to us) good that comes of it—perhaps not now but later, perhaps not to the one it happens to, but to *someone;* and only God, not man, is able to coordinate such intricate and delicate interactions among men. The best I can do is try to discern His Will and humbly submit to it.

I always thought that I was the only one who could possibly know what is good for me. In a sense this is at least partly true, but only among other humans, and it presupposes that I truly know what is good for me compared to them. In that situation, I am certainly the best judge; but God is an even *better* judge, and only He can see the long-range ripple effect of every choice or decision I make and every action I perform. If His overarching goal is to give each of us Eternal Life with Him and for us to participate through His Son in the family of His love, then, in our diabolically disordered world, when bad things happen (because the world is disordered, not God) He works ceaselessly to transform every evil to accomplish that overarching goal.

And yet, we fight Him tooth and nail at every moment, trying to prevent Him from achieving this wonderful goal! This is the self-destructive aspect of human nature that we psychiatrists so often encounter in our patients. The potential for self-ruination permeates every person's life.

My mother had been on a path of self-destruction, and it eventually led to her death from alcoholism. Yet, thank God, I was there at the end of her life and, even as a supposedly committed atheist (or so I told myself), I was able to make sure she had the necessary Last Rites of the Church. I strongly believe she is now with the Lord and happy, as my dream revealed to me. Her being able to receive this final sacrament was also a milestone on my own journey to faith, since that was the moment I abandoned atheism and became an agnostic, a much more rational position, which left me open for even more Truth and Grace to enter my life. It was another step in my own salvation.

When I murdered an innocent life through abortion, God was also busy transforming this horrific crime into a step in my own redemption. I firmly believe and trust that God has graciously forgiven me, though it has been harder to forgive myself. As for that innocent victim of my selfishness, can she be bereft of God's love and redemption? Never! I am sure that she is safely in the arms of our Lord and His Blessed Mother. When I confessed this sin and my overwhelming shame because of it, my priest and pastor urged me to go to the Blessed Mother and ask her what the name of the child was, and the name *Maria* came to me in prayer. That is the name by which I now think of this blessed child, whom I hope to meet someday. I will never fully understand the role that my baby and all the hundreds of thousands of aborted babies in the world play in God's plan—perhaps it is as victim souls to join with Christ's sacrifice on the cross so that others can be saved—but I have confidence that I will someday understand. And, miracle of miracles, God arranged for me to save another unwanted baby (whose mother, I thank God, did not make the same choice I had made) and so I was able to adopt my precious daughter Alexandra.

I see clearly now, in retrospect, that my obsession with space and space exploration was at least partly motivated by my desire to escape the inner turmoil of my own life. But even this part of my life taught me important lessons about psychological and spiritual denial. There is grace and goodness in the pursuit of exploration, but only when such exploration and risk is done for the Glory of God— not for the glory of an ideology or of man. Otherwise, it is mere self-gratification and self-deceit. Those space pioneers I have been privileged to meet who died in the service of advancing humanity are true heroes. Their lives made a difference in the history of the world. And yet, those who die for love of God as martyrs and who defend the Truth are even more majestic in the sacrifices they make, and are loved by Our Lord in a special way.

I also learned that as important as contributing to mankind's base of knowledge and his advancement into the boundless universe is, even more important is loving God and seeing God in each other. That is what life is all about, really. If your work allows you to help many others in the now or the future, that is an added bonus. But everyone honors their Father in heaven by doing the best at whatever it is they do in this life. A doctor isn't more important in God's eyes than a janitor. A politician isn't more important than a homeless person—not to God's way of thinking, anyway.

My reversion to Catholicism has led me to greatly desire the conversion of my two brothers and their families and to pray to our loving Father for them and all the people I know. Thus God, through me, is now working to get my family into paradise. I cannot do it without His grace, nor can they; but I will continue to pray for them and for the grace to make it happen.

As for my ex-husband, I sincerely hope that he finds true peace and happiness in his new marriage, something that I was not able to give him in our union—though I should have tried harder. I hope that he can forgive me one day for what I put him through during the divorce, since I bear a higher percentage of the blame in that matter. I freely and completely forgive him for any wrongs I felt were committed against me, and I wish him well. I see only now that the divorce and its consequences were a low point of my life; but it was that low point which strangely permitted me to rediscover my relationship with God. With Mary's rosary to assist, I finally appreciated how much I needed Him and how empty my life was without Him.

I find that it is now easy to freely and completely forgive any and all persons whom I have felt in my life "trespassed against me." My anger and bitterness have been extinguished even as I have finally found the love of my life and a soulmate in Jesus. Does that sound trite? People say it all the time, and it's because His love is a special kind of love that simply cannot be found in mere human relationships—a love that is undeterred by your faults and perseveres no matter what obstacles you might put in its way; a love that always has your best interests at heart, yet permits you the freedom to accept or reject it without alteration. That was the kind of love that I was so desperately seeking all my life as I restlessly moved from one relationship to another. God alone knows our true self and loves us in a way that is not possible from anyone else. This is not to diminish the love we have for others in our lives, but simply to recognize that no matter how much we love or are loved by another, God loves each of us even more. Only in Him does that restlessness that St. Augustine talked about find true ease.

There is a reason why Jesus gave us His Mother as His last action on the Cross. We need to be born again and be nurtured in the loving arms of a mother who can carry us proudly and lovingly to the Father. I was born again through Mary because I needed a mother's love. Without realizing it, I invited her into my life as a child with my child's devotion to the rosary. I chose her name for my confirmation name, Patricia Anne Marie Santy (it was also my earthly mother's middle name). In her mild and unobtrusive manner, she gently and continually nudged me in the direction of her beloved Son. She showed me by example how to discern and do the will of God. Ignoring my angry avowals of atheism, she knew my heart as a good mother does. And behind the bravado, my heart was broken. In anger, I lashed out at God in the way I unconsciously knew would hurt Him the most: by denying Him. He had died on the cross for me, and I was going to laugh in His face. I was going to prove that I didn't need Him or His Church. I was going to "be my own kind of winner" as I said in my poem from way back then.

> Since men are unprepared for a revelation of the heavenly image of Love, which is Christ Jesus Our Lord, God, in His mercy, has prepared on earth an image of love that is not Divine, but can lead to the Divine. Such is the role of His Mother. She can lift the fear, because her foot crushed the serpent of evil; she can do away with dread, because she stood at the foot of the Cross when human guilt was washed away and we were reborn in Christ.[26]

Mary understood the truth of me. She saw beyond the myth I made of myself to the real me, and she knew that her Son saw it too. She always knows the Truth, because she gave birth to the Truth. She understood long before I did, that in the deepest part of my being, I yearned and desperately wanted to believe in Truth, in Him. I desperately wanted to love and be loved. Why else would I so angrily denounce Him? Why bother to denounce someone you don't think exists? Why rage against a being that is only a figment

---

26 Sheen, Fulton (1952). *The World's First Love: Mary, Mother of God.* Ignatius Press, San Francisco. p. 198.

of humanity's imagination, if He doesn't exist? Clearly I thought He DID exist if I was able to be so angry at Him.

Because of her preservation from sin, Mary is not less human than you or I. This reality makes her even more human since she is what humans were meant to be and what humans will be when they cooperate fully with God. We were meant to be completely good and to never turn away from our Creator.

Mary led me to her Rosary and to the Garden itself. And, as I prayed on those beads, sometimes called "the Gospel on a string"— initially just to relax, then later to contemplate the mysteries of Jesus' and Mary's lives that go along with them—a subtle change began to take place within me. Grace and Truth entered my life, and I was no longer in the shadow of a cross, but in the light of God. I was on the side that wins, the side whose victory was confirmed the moment that Christ reconciled human nature to His Father.

St. Faustina's diaries record this message from Our Lord (1728): "Tell sinners that I am always waiting for them, that I listen intently to the beating of their heart…when will it beat for Me?"

I have read many books that discuss the "problem of evil," and I know that such a problem only can be asked in a world view in which God exists. If He doesn't exist, then the issue is moot and it is a pointless question, because good and evil don't exist either. I understand now, that bad things happen, not because God wills them to happen, but because ours is a broken and disordered world which became broken when man pitted his will against God's and imagined he could do better. God permits evil, yes. But wills it? No! Evil is by definition the turning away from God. Every time we turn away from God, we commit evil because justice demands that we acknowledge and listen to our Creator.

And imagine how impossible it would be for a human being to bring ultimate good out of every evil that transpired in the world, out of every sin committed by every other human being. God uses each of us, just as we are, to bring as many of us to Him as possible. He uses everything we do, for good or ill, for the same divine purpose. Even my fifty years of rebellion were surely used in some fashion I cannot imagine to help others—just as Satan and his angels' rebellion was and is being used to bring us all freely and without coercion back to Him forever. Hasn't this always been part of His plan? And in my own small, negligible way, I too, was a part of that magnificent plan from the beginning of all time.

How else can I possibly explain those persons who were touch-points in my life? Healers and patients; astronauts and lovers; family and friends. Even if they encountered me only briefly; even if they impacted me, or I them, only minutely; they all were guided by the gentle hands of my spiritual mother, whose mantle of protection I have always been under, and who unerringly has led her prodigal daughter back to the family of Father and Son.

How Mary must have grieved when I murdered the child in my womb and she carried the soul of that child to the Lord. How she must have grieved for both the child and for me. But with unspeakable tenderness she was able to lead me toward my daughter, not yet conceived in reality, but only within the Father's Divine Imagination.

How distressed she must have felt as I made one wrong choice after another in men; knowing that the man I was truly seeking was her Son, and that all He wanted was to give me His love, and all I had to do was accept it.

How painful it must have been for her (for she is human and not divine) to watch as I made mistake after mistake and followed my own, often self-destructive will instead of the will of the Father. "Do whatever he tells you," were the last words she spoke in the Gospels. And she has been saying the same thing in apparition after apparition, always pointing to her Son who leads us to the Father, and through whom we know the Father.

How delighted and amused she must have been when I found my old rosary, or when I went to Fatima and it gave me an excuse to pray again on those beloved beads. I can almost see her and her Son joyfully smiling as I struggled to pretend that the prayers were a type of Zen meditation. Remembering her promises to those who pray the rosary, she must have frequently interceded on my behalf to the Father and Son, whose grace in my life finally led to my leap across the chasm that separated me from faith and Him.

And when everything shifted, when the pattern of the world reset itself somehow for me, how suddenly disinterested I felt in the things which I had once valued and enjoyed. How worthless and empty seemed all my accomplishments in this world! How mean-ingless were the accolades and riches that I had accumulated over my lifetime! Nothing mattered anymore like it had. I was in charge of a large medical department. I no longer cared about that or being important. I was a well-thought-of psychiatrist. It felt empty and boring. Oh, I knew I still had to live in this world, but I didn't care about it in the same way as before.

Everywhere I turned I could see now an evil that was stalking mankind. Every part of me, every molecule of my being just wanted to know more about Jesus with whom I had fallen in love. He was now my Beloved. And I wanted to know EVERYTHING I possibly could about Him. I had thousands of years of writings to familiarize myself with so I could learn all that had been written and thought about Jesus; and even if I were able to process all of it, it would not be possible to know or understand everything.

Shortly after I came back to the faith I had the dream about the church in the desert and the knight. That dream was especially pro-phetic for me because at the time, I had never actually read the Bible, so I had no idea what "the 144,000" meant or what the knight was talking about. But after reading Revelation, it became clear to me that this dream effectively encapsulated my entire life. I had entered a church in the world and in the confessional had gone to sleep for a long time, abandoning myself to sin. But eventually I woke up to another world, God's world, and it lay stretched out before me like another planet. The knight was my guide, one of the chosen of God to rescue those who had been lost. I wondered if the 144,000 might also be the army of the Immaculata—Mary's militia—that St. Maximilian Kolbe founded in 1917, close to the same time as she was appearing in Fatima to three small children. The knights of this order consider Mary's rosary as their spiritual sword:

> Shortly after the rosary was given to the world, the Dominicans and members of other mendicant religious orders began to wear the rosary on the left side of their habit in imitation of knights. Most people are right-handed, and knights would wear their sword on their left side for easy access when drawing the sword out of its sheath.[27]

27 Calloway, Donald H. (2019) *10 Wonders of the Rosary.* Marian Press; Stock-bridge, MA; p.27

In the dream, I had particularly noted the knight's beautiful sword; but I wondered if it was not like the sword of Jean Parisot de Valette during the Great Siege of Malta (1565):

> In this siege, the Muslim armada consisted of more than 40,000 men, while the Catholic army consisted of only about 6000 men. The odds were greatly against the Catholics. Miraculously, under the leadership of Jean Parisot de Valette, the grand master of the Sovereign Military Order of St. John (the Knights of Malta), the Catholic army was able to defend the island and repel the Muslims. While the Catholic army suffered many casualties, the Muslim army suffered the loss of more than 30,000 men.
>
> The most fascinating aspect of the Great Siege of Malta involves the sword used by Jean Parisot de Valette during the battle. In preparation for the confrontation with the Muslims, de Valette went to a blacksmith and commissioned a special sword. He requested that a rosary be engraved on the blade of his sword! He knew what the rosary was, and he wasn't afraid to show it in battle. The rosary was his spiritual weapon.[28]

The dream also was symbolic of my change in perspective and my newly-awakened desire to defend the Church against all the modern and postmodern attacks and heresies that are bringing her into a period of desolation. Compared to this desire, all my academic achievements tasted like "straw" and meant little. I had a very good idea what St. Thomas Aquinas had felt after his own encounter with the Lord. This prophetic dream was one of many that I subsequently had over the next several years.

Or, What's a Heaven For?

She was applying for college and this was the day of the interview. The driver brought her to a very large, rambling mansion that looked like a house built in the 1940's or earlier. It had porticos, porches, extensions and many fireplaces as witnessed by the chimneys.

"This is the college?" she wondered, and just then, someone opened the car door for her and said, "I will be your guide today. Let me show you around."

She was fascinated by the house and couldn't wait to explore it with her charming guide. They went up the stairs to a large wooden

---

28 Ibid, pp.32-33.

door and entered. The entrance was lovely. There were flowers everywhere, fresh and fragrant.

"Let's go to the right wing," her guide said. And they proceeded down a long hall which seemed to have many doors. He opened the first door and she peeked inside and instantly was delighted, like a child.

"It's all decorated in Christmas!" she cried out. He smiled. The room displayed a very traditional Christmas décor, all red and green. A tree, decorated beautifully, was in the far corner next to the fireplace, which was blazing away. People sat on the floor opening presents. It smelled like pine and oranges. The guide closed the door and led her to the next room.

Another Christmas scene! This room had snow and everyone was busy building snowmen and decorating Christmas wreaths. It was all white and red. At her beaming smile, because she loved Christmas more than any other time of the year, he answered her unasked question.

"Many of the rooms are Christmas-themed," he told her.

"Oh, that's wonderful! I like this college very much." He smiled. "Would you like to see the room prepared for you?"

"Oh yes," she said. "Is it decorated in Christmas?"

"All the common rooms are, but your personal room is decorated for you specially." He led her down the hall for some minutes until they came to a corner, and then he opened the door of the corner room. Her response was even more delighted. "This is mine??" The guide, who she noticed for the first time seemed to have wings on his back, said, "If you like it."

"Of course I like it! It's wonderful, everything I've always wanted!" She gazed in disbelief at the incredible scene. At the far end was a large window, looking out at the ocean. The walls were covered with books carefully arranged in bookshelves that extended upwards for as far as she could see. There was a soft, comfortable-looking chair by the window with a footstool. "Oh, just look at all the books!" she said excitedly. "They are all yours to explore," the guide said. You can go as often as you like to the

Christmas rooms. It will take you a very long time to explore them all, and to read the books." He smiled again. "You will have a very long time."

"But how can this be a college?" she asked, somewhat perplexed at what was happening.

"Your Father's house has many mansions, and this one is prepared for you."

Pilgrimage

Soon after coming back to belief in God, I found I wanted to pay my respects to Him and His Mother in some special manner. This is what pilgrimages are all about. In the Catholic tradition, pilgrimages have always been considered a special way of honoring God and bringing the pilgrim spiritually closer to Him.

The first pilgrimage I signed up for was to go to Mexico to see Our Lady of Guadalupe, whom I spoke about in Chapter 5. I was curious to see the famous and miraculous tilma of Our Lady which is in the Basilica there, and I wished to truly honor Mary by my visit. I signed up to go on a pilgrimage led by Dr. Taylor Marshall, a Catholic philosopher, of whose New St. Thomas Institute I had become a member in order to study Catholic philosophy and theology.

The story of the tilma of Our Lady of Guadalupe is not as well known in the United States as it should be. It is so miraculous that it has the power to convert anyone who takes the time to research its history with an open mind, like John in his Gospel when he entered the tomb and saw it empty with the burial shroud and face cloth folded nearby and wrote, "He saw and he believed." (John 20:8)

The actual tilma (or cloak) hangs in the back of the Basilica of Guadalupe behind the altar, and it absolutely dominates the entire church, even though it is only the size of a human cloak and the Basilica itself is huge, holding up to ten thousand people.

I can't possibly explain the impact that seeing the image of Our Blessed Mother had on me. The actual tilma is preserved behind unbreakable glass, and pilgrims can go back and forth on a motorized walkway to gaze at the image. I found I could not take my eyes

Interior of the Shrine of Our Lady of Guadalupe, Mexico.

off it. The image was imprinted on a plant-based garment 500 years ago, and yet it looks fresh and bright and can be seen from anywhere inside the Basilica. The image is actual physical proof of Mary's apparition to Juan Diego in 1531. Amazingly, during the Cristero War in Mexico in the 1920's, someone tried to blow up the image, which at the time was hanging in the old cathedral and had far less protection than it has today. A bomb was hidden in flowers placed below the image. Massive destruction ensued when it exploded… but the tilma was miraculously unharmed.

One other pilgrimage I embarked on was to travel to Israel and walk where Jesus and the Apostles walked. Like most pilgrimages to Israel, this was an arduous trip, since it crammed many important sites into a short period of time. Galilee, Capernaum, the Jordan River, the old city of Jerusalem, the Holy Sepulcher, the Upper Room, the Kedron Valley, Gethsemane, Bethlehem, Nazareth, Cana, Mt. Tabor…. Fortunately, Israel is a very small country (about the size of New Jersey) and even a short pilgrimage is time enough to see many holy sites. It was a stunning experience to be in the places where Jesus performed His miracles and where He lived and died and was buried, then rose again.

These two pilgrimages set the stage for my new life in Christ and filled me with zeal and reverence. But God was not done with me yet.

Witness

I settled into my new-found faith in God somewhat uncomfortably. My family was incredulous and thought it was a passing thing and that I would get over it. Friends expressed some disappointment in my becoming so irrational and pointed out that I was hardly saint material, which was true in many ways. My first few months going back to the Catholic Church were very lonely, as I did not know anyone at the church, and unlike many Protestant churches, there was no welcoming committee to make you feel at home. I saw an announcement in the church bulletin about needing people for "adoration." I didn't know what that was, but it was for an hour a week, so I thought I would call the number and find out. Maybe this was something I could do to get to know more people from church.

Adoration is the term used for spending time with the Blessed Sacrament, which Catholics firmly believe is the True Body and Blood of Jesus. After the hosts are consecrated at Mass, they are kept in the Tabernacle, which is like the "holy of holies" in the old Jewish Temple. But on a regular basis, one of the hosts is placed in a beautiful container (called a monstrance) and taken out of the Tabernacle for the purpose of adoration. As Jesus said to Peter, James and John in Gethsemane prior to His Passion, "Could you not watch one hour with me?" (Mk 14:34)

Different churches have different hours of adoration; some even have it 24/7. There must always be a person present when the Blessed Sacrament is exposed.

This beautiful devotion to Our Lord was an inspiration for me. I started participating in adoration for one hour a week on Fridays, and soon that hour of contemplation and peace became the best part of my week.

One day as I was leaving the Adoration Chapel after my hour was up, a woman who was entering stopped me and cheerfully started talking to me. I didn't know her, but she seemed to know me, and after we had chatted for a brief time, she impulsively invited me to join a small group of women who were meeting to discuss theology books every week. I was ecstatic! I was finally getting to know some of the people at church. Little did I realize that this small group of women was to become one of the most important relationships in my life. Annie, Carol, Dori, Sophia and I have met weekly now for many years and my life would be bereft without these women, my sisters, in it. Never having had a sister (let alone four of them!) they were and are very special to me.

It was a first small step for me into the faith community. Annie, whom I met first, seemed to know everyone and took it upon herself to introduce me around. I started regularly meeting with her and Carol; then Dori and Sophia joined us as we discussed various Catholic books in-depth. I felt strongly that this study and all the readings from the New St. Thomas Institute were God's way of preparing me for something, and this coincided with my own sense that there was something I needed to do, some service I could render to God through the Church. I started praying for some direction and

A monstrance in which the
Sacred Host is exposed for adoration.

almost immediately, I received a letter in the mail from the pastor of the Church, Monsignor Patrick McCormick (Fr. Pat), inviting me to become a member of the Healing Prayer Ministry.

And so, I answered that letter and began to take the training necessary to become a part of the healing prayer ministry. As a physician and psychiatrist, it was a perfect fit. Little did I know the surprise that the Lord had prepared for me.

During a training session one weekend, I received a miraculous healing through the Holy Spirit. I cannot describe it in any other manner, and neither can the doctors.

To tell you about it, I have to go back to when I was a rambunctious 3-year-old living in the old house with the upstairs apartment with my parents, while my grandparents and my mother's sister and her husband and child lived downstairs. There was a long narrow stairway up to this apartment, and to prevent my falling, my parents put up a gate. Despite that effort to protect me, I tumbled down those stairs one day, breaking several bones and tearing most of the muscles that control the movements in my eyes, particularly the right eye. The accident led to several long hospitalizations and surgeries on the eyes to repair the damage. I had nightmares for years about the surgeries because in those days, children were basically tied down on the operating table and nothing that was going to happen would be explained to them. I remember screaming and screaming as a large black object was placed over my mouth, and then nothing. I woke up from the surgery in total darkness, my arms tied on each side to the bed. Not understanding what was going on, I started to whimper, thinking I was dead. I only had the smallest concept of what death was at that age, but I believed I had been "bad" and was being punished forever for something I had done. With this kind of traumatic experience at a young age, it makes sense that I eventually became a doctor and then a psychiatrist as an attempt to understand what had happened to me. I can still hear my father's soothing voice in that hospital room, telling me I was going to be all right, when my cries alerted him that I was awake after the surgery.

What followed was a long rehabilitation of my eyes with eye patches, exercises and persistent double vision. Two years later and after multiple surgeries, I was finally able to focus my eyes fairly normally, but I had to wear thick-prismed glasses to be able to see the world in focus. I looked so strange as a child in those big black, thick glasses that my grandfather and my family referred to me for years as "the little professor."

Since then, I have had to have the same eye muscle surgery multiple times to make my eyes able to focus as the muscles around the eye would slowly stretch until they tore apart again, requiring more surgery. Attempts to repair the muscles were less and less successful. The last surgery was in 2001 and I was told then that there could be no more surgeries as the muscle in my right eye was now too fragile and too ripped up by all the surgical stitches over the years, so there could be no chance of repair.

I resigned myself to reading with just the one eye and closing my right eye.

During the healing prayer ministry training exercises, someone suggested that I volunteer to be prayed over since I was having a particularly difficult time seeing clearly even with new glasses. I had recovered from cataract surgery two months earlier; and, while this improved my distance vision, I still could not make my eyes focus and was wearing an eye patch again. I was reluctant about being prayed over, but finally consented. Cheerfully, I told my group, "Well, anything is possible with God." It never occurred to me that perhaps my injury at age 3 was part of His larger plan.

The team prayed, asking the Holy Spirit specifically to heal my right eye muscle as I sat there with my eyes closed and glasses off. Suddenly I felt a strange movement of that always-problematic right eye. When I opened my eyes and looked around, I could hardly believe it. My eyes were working perfectly together—even without those awful glasses. I could suddenly see small details of things; a blade of grass outside the window came into focus, then a leaf on a tree. Inside the church, for the first time I could see the details of the crucifix behind the altar. And, I could read with both eyes! How and why had this extraordinary thing happened to me? What did it mean? I simply can't describe everything that was going through my mind, but I felt a tremendous peace and an overwhelming gratitude. When the Holy Spirit gives you a gift like this, it is not done solely for your benefit, but for the benefit of all the members of the Church.

The doctors were puzzled and couldn't explain why the muscle was now functioning. They suggested that perhaps something in my brain's vision center might have been altered. But I knew God had worked a miracle through the prayer team. And I understood that this miraculous healing was not about me or even for me: it was a demonstration of God's power and glory, which almost all of us have forgotten in modern times. This miracle convinced me that God was calling me to be involved in healing in His name and to give witness to Him. Not long after that I was asked to participate in the Diocesan Healing and Deliverance Ministry team which was tasked with doing deliverance and exorcisms by the bishop of the diocese. This is how I was introduced to the idea of spiritual warfare, a concept that I had never considered.

St. Paul wrote in his letter to the Ephesians:

Brothers and sisters, finally, be strong in the Lord and in the strength of his might. Put on the full armor of God so as to be able to resist the devil's tactics. For it is not against human enemies that we have to struggle, but against the principalities and the ruling forces who are masters of the darkness in this world, the spirit of evil in the heavens.

That is why you must take up all God's armor, or you will not be able to put up any resistance on the evil day, or stand your ground even though you exert yourselves to the full. (Ep 6:10-13)

Father Pat asked me to give witness to my healing for the entire congregation at my parish, Holy Spirit, which I did, although I was terrified in a way that I had never been before while speaking publicly. I gave my witness, and I can only hope that my experience of a real miracle healing in my life was a source of hope and inspiration for anyone who might be suffering from the "devil's tactics" in their own life.

Have I mentioned how significant the Blessed Virgin was during this time? I know she was instrumental in my becoming a member of the Healing and Deliverance Ministry and in my own healing because I had recently performed the steps of consecration to Jesus through Mary as outlined in Father Gaitley's book, *33 Days to Morning Glory,* which we were reading in my theology group. Part of this consecration is asking Our Holy Mother to take any of the merits from our prayers and sacrifices and to use them for the intentions of her Immaculate Heart:

[Pope John Paul II] goes on to explain that consecration to the Immaculate Heart of Mary means "returning to the Cross of the Son." It means bringing the world and all its problems and suffering to "the pierced Heart of the Savior" and thus "back to the very source of its Redemption." It means bringing the world, through Mary, to Divine Mercy! The power of the Redemption, the power of merciful Love, is always greater than man's sin and the "sin of the world" and is "infinitely superior to the whole range of evil in man and the world."

Now, Mary knows the power of the Redemption, the power of merciful Love, better than anyone. In fact, John Paul says she knows it "more than any other heart in the whole universe, visible and invisible." Therefore, she calls us not only to conversion but "to accept her motherly help to return to the source of Redemption." For again Mary's task is to bring us to the Fountain of Mercy, to the pierced side of Christ, to his Merciful Heart.

Essentially, then, consecrating ourselves to Mary "means accepting her help to offer ourselves and the whole of mankind to the infinitely Holy God."[29]

During the persecution of Christians in 250 AD by the Emperor Decius, a hymn to the Blessed Virgin Mary was very popular. It is one of the earliest prayers ever found that is dedicated to Our Holy Mother and in it, we ask for her protection from evil.

Sub Tuum Praesidium

Sub tuum praesidium confugimus, Sancta Dei Genetrix.
Nostras deprecationes ne despicias in necessitatibus,
sed a periculis cunctis libera nos semper,
Virgo gloriosa et benedicta.

We Fly to Thy Protection
We fly to Thy protection, O Holy Mother of God;
Do not despise our petitions in our necessities,
but deliver us always from all dangers,
O Glorious and Blessed Virgin.

---

29 Gaitley, Michael. (2013) *33 Days to Morning Glory.* Marian Press; Stockbridge, MA; p. 103

CHAPTER 9

FINALLY HOME

Sister

Isolated, my dear
You pray sincerely but
Wonder if He is there to
Hear

The world is your convent
And you are chaste but
Long to break the vows
That keep you bound to pleasure
And lay your soul to waste

The Family of Christ

Christians believe, and St. Paul has said, that we are all one in Christ (Gal 3:28). But what does this really mean? In John 6:57 during the Bread of Life discourse, which led to many of Jesus' followers abandoning Him because it was too hard for them to understand, Jesus said, "As the living Father sent me, and I live because of the Father, so he who eats me will live because of me." Now this is interesting because Jesus says that He lives because of the Father. So, the communion of Jesus with the Father in the spiritual realm is parallel in the physical (human) realm to eating the consecrated bread and drinking the consecrated wine, transformed into the Body and Blood of Jesus during the Holy Sacrifice of the Mass. In the first case, the Father gives life to His Son; in the second, the Son gives life to us. Thus, when we eat the transubstantiated bread of Holy Communion, we become one with the body of Christ, who is one with the Father. Now, in the family of the Father and Son, there is another Person, the Holy Spirit. The Holy Spirit is the Giver of Life who proceeds from the Father to the Son, and from the Son to the Father. These three Persons in One God are the Family of God. Think of that! God is a family!

In the human realm, Jesus also was part of a family, His Mother Mary and His foster father Joseph. Jesus bequeathed His Mother Mary to all of humanity while He was on the cross. He also told us in the Gospels how we can become united to Him (be "in Him and He in us") through the Eucharistic Feast. This "Supper of the Lamb" corresponds to the communion of love between the Father and Son in Heaven; and it enables us, as physical human beings, to participate in that spiritual communion by becoming part of the Body of Christ in the physical sacrament during Holy Mass. In this way, we are mystically able to participate in the love between Father and Son. This is incredibly wonderful! It seems to me that this is one of the reasons that it is so important for families to eat together on a regular basis. The very act of eating, taking in nourishment, is the human equivalent of the spiritual nourishment that the Father, Son and Holy Spirit are continually exchanging. We are not spiritual beings, but God has made us in His image, and exchanging food is one of the major ways that we humans exchange love in the physical world. In Italian families (as well as in other ethnicities) the constant exhortation to "Eat! *Mangia!*" is a clear expression of a mother's love. And, of course, Jesus called Himself "the bread of life."

The mystical connection between the Family of God and the extended Family of Christ (of which we all can choose to be a part) is one of the great wonders of Christian belief. Spiritual beings have no need of sexuality to create life, but we physical beings, having been made in the image of God, are male and female through which we can imitate God's creation and co-create life. Mary was special as she conceived of the Holy Spirit (as the Angel declared unto her) and brought forth not only the spiritual Son, but also the physical Son of God in a hypostatic union that cannot be fully understood, but which actually happened.

Thus, we are one in Christ Jesus; Mary is our spiritual mother, and her spouse, Joseph, is our spiritual father.

Third Order

Several years after my reversion, one other event happened that is of note. One day I was reading a book that made reference to St. Catherine of Siena. Not being familiar with that particular saint, I quickly looked her up on the Internet.

The saint's biography referred to her as a "Third Order Dominican," and puzzled as to what that meant, and I had to look that up also. I read:

> Lay Dominicans are men and women, singles and couples living a Christian life with a Dominican spirituality in the secular world. They find inspiration following the same spiritual path taken by many saints, blesseds, and other holy men and women throughout the 800-year history of the Dominican Order. The life of a Dominican layperson is all about having a passion for the Word of God. It is about committing one's self to a community of like-minded brothers and sisters that immerse themselves in the Word of God. There are Lay Dominican Provinces all around the world.
> (*Quoted from Wikipedia*)

I'd never heard of such a thing. Wasn't Catherine always pictured wearing a full Dominican habit? I felt a rising excitement as I read. Catholic tradition has it that the rosary in its current form was presented to St. Dominic, the founder of the Dominican Order, by Our Blessed Lady in 1208.

Dominic Guzmán was a Spanish priest who traveled throughout France preaching against the Albigensian heresy, but he and his fellow priests' efforts gained few conversions and even fewer followers.

[The heresy] was based on a dual view of the world similar to that of the Manicheans of the 3rd century; namely that there are two supreme beings, a good god who created the spirit world, and an evil god who created the material world. The spiritual world is essentially good, and the material world (including the human body) is essentially evil. The evil god (Satan) imprisoned spirits in material bodies, so whatever one can do to be released from that prison (including suicide) is good. Since matter is evil, marriage and the procreation of mankind are evil. The proponents of this heresy rejected Catholic belief regarding the Trinity, the Incarnation, the sacraments, hell and purgatory, but believed in the transmigration of souls. Christ was not truly a man, nor therefore, was Mary truly the Mother of God. The crucifixion, death and resurrection of Christ were only illusions, and the whole concept of the cross in the Christian life was rejected.

Its rapid growth was nourished, among other things, by the moral laxity and worldliness of the clergy. In addition, most of the nobility fostered the heresy because of their hope to take over the lands and goods of the Church.[30]

Tradition has it that Dominic was praying near Toulouse in 1208, asking God for help in his battle against the Albigensians, and that he was favored with a vision of the Virgin Mary who told him to preach her Psalter.

It was common in the time of Dominic to use a string of beads or rope knots to keep track of prayers. In the early 13th century, the Hail Mary prayer did not exist as we pray it today. Only the first part which came directly from the Gospels was used (*"Hail, Mary, full of grace. The Lord is with thee. Blessed art thou among women, and blessed is the fruit of your womb."*). The second part of the prayer was not added until much later, and the word "Jesus" was added in the 14th century. What was called the "Marian Psalter"

---

30 Duffner, Fr. Paul. "In Defense of a Tradition." https://www.rosarycenter.org/in-defense-of-a-tradition/

*St. Dominic de Guzmán, founder of the Dominican Order,
receiving the Rosary from the Blessed Virgin*

came originally from the practice of monks in monasteries praying all 150 Psalms in the Bible during their regular prayers. Since the Bible was not available to those in the laity (since there were no printing presses, copies of the Bible were handwritten and thus very few and precious), laypersons imitated this monks' routine by praying the Our Father prayer instead of each Psalm (so the beads were called Paternoster beads). Later, a parallel prayer of saying 150 Hail Mary's along with the Creed at the beginning and the Our Father in between each decade, or ten Hail Mary's, was established. This latter practice was called the "Marian Psalter." The idea of each Hail Mary having an associated "mystery" that referred back to events in the life of Christ and Mary is said to have been given to Dominic when the Virgin appeared to him. Eventually the 150 Hail Mary's evolved into the concept of a "rosary" of five decades, and for each decade the person praying would contemplate a mystery.

MYSTERIES OF THE ROSARY

JOYFUL	LUMINOUS	SORROWFUL	GLORIOUS
Mondays & Saturdays & Sundays of Advent	Thursdays	Tuesdays & Fridays Sundays of Lent	Wednesdays & Sundays
1. The Annunciation	1. Baptism in the Jordan	1. Agony in the Garden	1. The Resurrection
2. The Visitation	2. Wedding at Cana	2. Scourging at the Pillar	2. The Ascension
3. The Nativity	3. Proclamation of the Kingdom of God	3. Crowning with Thorns	3. Descent of the Holy Spirit
4. The Presentation	4. Transfiguration	4. Carrying of the Cross	4. The Assumption
5. Finding of Jesus in the Temple	5. Institution of the Eucharist	5. Crucifixion	5. The Coronation

THINK OF ONE MYSTERY WHILE SAYING A COMPLETE DECADE

While some dispute the historical account of the presentation of the Rosary by Our Lady to St. Dominic, many theologians and Popes have upheld this understanding through the centuries. History confirms that St. Dominic was the first to preach and teach the rosary as a form of meditative prayer, and the first to see the benefits reaped from meditation upon its mysteries.

As I read the history of the Dominicans, I remembered my childhood desire to become a nun. I was strongly drawn to Dominican spirituality, which had a special devotion to Mary and the rosary, as well as a deep appreciation of teaching, learning, meditation, and prayer. Was the calling I experienced as a child re-emerging? Wasn't I now too old to contemplate doing this? But it felt right. I decided to ask my pastor, Fr. Pat, for his opinion.

Fr. Pat was very helpful and assured me that my age was no problem. He confided that he, himself was a Third Order Carmelite, in addition to being a priest. He suggested the Carmelites or Franciscans to me as options, but I felt that the charism of the Dominicans was right for me. Thomas Aquinas had been a Dominican and I admired him greatly. His lucid and comprehensive writings in philosophy and theology had been largely responsible for convincing me intellectually of the existence of God. Additionally, the Marian traditions further confirmed that all the threads of my life were leading me to the Dominicans.

I researched online where the closest Lay Dominican community was, and was delighted to discover that it was not very far away! Within a few months, I had applied to join the community and participated in several meetings. I was sure that this was what God (and Mary!) wanted me to do. I entered the inquiry and then the novitiate stage of Lay Formation, and after two years of supervised study, I was fully accepted into the St. Hyacinth Community of the Western Province of the Holy Name of Jesus

In 2014, writing in the online journal *First Things*, C.C. Pecknold offered "The Dominican Option" as an alternative to the "Benedict Option." In the latter, one is encouraged to withdraw from the world in order to preserve faith and civilization from barbarianism, while the former is "very much engaged with the world—an evangelistic witness which is joyful, intellectually serious, expansive and charitable."

The pieces of the puzzle of my life had mysteriously arranged themselves into a rosary pattern, and I had come full circle. The vows one takes as a lay Dominican are not binding in the same way they are for a nun or priest, but the intent is to dedicate one's life to practicing the Dominican spirituality and spreading the good news in the world. I took as my patron saint and guide, Thomas Aquinas, from whom I learned so much.

God is so good and faithful! It is amazing to me that I am now in a religious order, and one that has produced many holy saints. May I live up to that tradition, Lord!

One of my dear friends and sisters in Christ, a very devout Catholic, attended my profession ceremony to cheer me on. During my vow, she herself felt a calling and has now entered the Third Order as a novice.

St. Thomas Aquinas, pray for us.

Excerpt of St. Thomas' Prayer to Our Lady

O most blessed and sweet Virgin Mary,
Mother of God, filled with all tenderness,
Daughter of the most high King,
Lady of the Angels,
Mother of all the faithful,
On this day and all the days of my life,
I entrust to your merciful heart my body and my soul,
all my acts, thoughts, choices, desires, words, deeds,
my entire life and death,
so that, with your assistance, all may be ordered to the good
according to the will of your beloved Son, our Lord Jesus Christ....

From your beloved Son...
request for me the grace to resist firmly
the temptations of the world, the flesh and the devil....
My most holy Lady,
I also beseech you to obtain for me
true obedience and true humility of heart
So that I may recognize myself truly
as a sinner—wretched and weak—
and powerless, without the grace and help of my Creator
and without your holy prayers....

Obtain for me as well,
O most sweet Lady,
true charity with which from the depths of my heart
I may love your most holy Son, our Lord Jesus Christ,
and, after Him,
love you above all other things....
Grant, O Queen of Heaven,
that ever in my heart
I may have fear and love alike

for your most sweet Son....
I pray also that, at the end of my life, you, Mother without
compare,
Gate of Heaven and Advocate of sinners....
will protect me with your great piety and mercy....
And obtain for me, through the blessed and glorious Passion of
your Son
and through your own intercession,
received in hope, the forgiveness of all my sins.
When I die in your love and His love,
may you direct me into the way of salvation and blessedness.
Amen.

Dreams of My Mother

Mary most blessed, Mother of God and my mother: the Father has painted you perfectly. You were a dream in His mind from the beginning of time. With perfect love He crafted you to bear His Son into the world of man. With perfect love, His Son gave you to us at the moment of His precious sacrifice.

> Most of us are a minus sign, in the sense that we do not fulfill the high hopes the Heavenly Father has for us. But Mary is the equal sign. The ideal that God had for her, that she is, and in the flesh. The model and the copy are perfect...the melody of her life played just as it was written. Mary was thought, conceived, and planned as the equal sign between ideal and history, thought and reality, hope and realization.[31]

Sometimes it feels like following Jesus is such hard work. In our imperfect state, we sin over and over again. It is hard to imagine a real, live person who was sinless from her conception on throughout her life—one who was perfectly aligned with the Will of God such that her every thought and action conformed to that Will.

Mary is the proof that our human nature is capable of good-ness and perfect holiness. She is a sign of hope that each of us can also align ourselves with the Will of God in all that we do. Her path was not an easy one, and she understood it would not be easy from the moment Simeon told her a sword would pierce her heart.

---

31 Sheen, Fulton (1952) *The World's First Love: Mary, the Mother of God.* Ignatius Press, San Francisco; p 17.

She completely shared in the suffering of her Son during His Passion, and the sorrow she must have experienced at His crucifixion is unimaginable. Yet, she accepted it as God's will as she accepted everything in her life. As a mother and a psychiatrist, I know that to witness such a horrific death—especially that of your beloved child—has the power to destroy a soul. Yet, Mary's soul always magnified the Lord. Her life of obedience with its suffering always conformed itself to the will of her Lord, and this is the pattern that many great saints have followed through the ages.

One of those saints who were profoundly influenced by Mary was the stigmatic, St. Padre Pio, to whom I have a special devotion. St. Pio credited Mary with healing him when he was deathly ill. From that time on he cheerfully suffered for her Son. Pio is a popular saint because he lived through most of the 20th century, and he was well-known not only because he bore the rare stigmata, but also because he was able to read people's souls. My grandmother considered him her favorite saint. Padre Pio often stated that his real work would be to help his "children" when he made it to heaven, and he is often invoked for special intercessions.

In my mission to bring my own child back to Christ, I have often asked for both St. Padre Pio's and for Mary's intercession. One day, during the first week of a new job that my daughter started, she came home from work for lunch tearful and distressed. "I can't do this, Mom," she told me. "It's too hard. I'm going to quit." I hardly knew what to say.

My daughter is a restless soul. She had been unhappy in all her previous jobs because she felt they were "going nowhere." Then she was offered this new job with a full salary and benefits and with a path to other opportunities. When she left lunch to return to work and presumably give notice, I fervently prayed a rosary with a special prayer request to St. Pio to help her make the right decision.

When Alexandra came home from work that evening, she was all smiles and informed me that she felt much calmer and better about the duties of the job. "I know I can do it." Her turnabout was remarkable. As an afterthought, she said, "You know, the strangest thing happened, Mom. I'm the person who receives all the mail each day and one of my jobs is to open each piece and give it to the appropriate person. Well, a letter came in this afternoon that was

only addressed to the company with no specific person's name on it. So I opened and read it. I thought you'd be interested because it was a prayer to one of your favorite saints! I think his name is Padre Pio."

Then she then showed me the note inside the letter and the envelope. There was no return address, and it had been posted several days before, simply addressed to the company she worked for. Inside was a prayer to Padre Pio typed on a small piece of paper!

> *Dear Padre Pio,*
> *From your place in heaven, please*
> *petition the Lord Jesus*
> *to watch over, bless and protect my family*
> *and all my loved ones.*
> *Through your holy intercession,*
> *I especially ask today for the grace of*
> *peace and good judgment. Amen.*

Our Lord works in mysterious ways, and through His Mother and His saints, we are blessed beyond measure*! "Give yourself up into the arms of your Heavenly Mother. She will take good care of your soul,"* says St. Pio.

Mary was the herald of the beginning of Christ's ministry (*"Do whatever tells you"*) and its end (*"Behold your Mother"*). She was present during the Passion, Resurrection and Ascension, as well as at the birth of the Church at Pentecost; and she will help guide the One, Holy, Catholic and Apostolic Church through whatever storms and trials may come until the end. Hers is the Blessed Womb through which we can be reborn in Christ. You are never isolated from her intercession, help or protection.

Saints and Sinners

Philosopher and mathematician Blaise Pascal said: "There are only two kinds of people we can call reasonable: either those who serve God with their whole heart because they know Him, or those who search after Him with all their heart because they do not know Him." Having been the latter kind and now transformed to the former, I completely agree with the mathematician.

I was and am a sinner, as these pages attest. I have few redeeming qualities, except perhaps an openness to Truth and a willingness to follow it wherever it takes me. Many years passed before I finally could appreciate that Truth (capital T) is a *person*, mainly because I was so intoxicated by the person of myself.

My journey with Mary has been a long and convoluted one. Its twists and turns have humbled me and shamed me many times. For most of the voyage, I did not even recognize her handiwork, but she has remained faithful nonetheless—as her Son is faithful—to a lonely little girl who loved her. She knew my heart as a child; she knew my longings and my turmoil, and like a good mother, she nurtured me and tolerated my foolish and self-destructive impulses, always gently steering me toward Jesus.

The child recognized in Mary the kind of mother I wanted to have and the kind of person I wanted to be. How lucky for me, then, that Jesus bequeathed her to me!

Saying this is not meant to disrespect my earthly mother, but rather to forgive her because she herself needed the same kind of mother, as do we all. I shall never fully appreciate on this side of life all the sadness and hopelessness in Mom's heart that led her to the poor decisions she made in her life. I know some of them, because despite everything, I realize that I am more like her than I want to believe. There but for the grace of God go I. Like her, I was on a search for love and could have easily ended up sad and lonely and self-destructive.

What made me different from her, I wondered? Mom went to Catholic school through high school and was considered very bright academically. Both she and her sister Pauline were predicted by the nuns who taught them to have great futures. I think that early in her life she learned that she could use her sexuality to get what she wanted from men and that this knowledge proved to be her undoing spiritually. She knew how to be helpless and make men take care of her. One of my vivid memories of my mother is her excessively long nails (we are talking 1½ inches long), which made her practically disabled when using her hands (except for typing at which she was a wiz). God gave her talent and looks. But because of the brokenness in her own family and her narcissism and emotionality, she squandered her talent and became obsessed with men and the pursuit of her passions. Perhaps the competition with her sister Pauline drove her in this direction. She both loved and hated her older sister; she was envious and contemptuous at the same time.

Mom did arrange for me and my brothers to be baptized and confirmed (for which I am truly grateful), but she was somewhat *laissez-faire* about her soul, and after her divorce from my father, I don't believe she attended Mass regularly despite graduating from a Catholic school. When she then married Glen, the local priest would not absolve her in confession unless she was repentant and did not plan to live with her second husband. This, of course she would never do and I think she stopped going to church entirely at that point in her life. That seems to be the time when things really started to go downhill for her. Glen had extramarital affairs (just as he did with her) and she couldn't handle it. She started drinking excessively, and the booze became her primary coping mechanism when she and Glen divorced. She supported herself as an administrative secretary for a Catholic hospital, but she was openly resentful of Catholicism during the latter part of her life.

I loved my mother despite everything and I felt very sorry for her. She and my father called me Patty Ann my entire life, and that nickname always endeared them both to me. But I never felt they knew or understood me. Of course, I didn't really understand them, either. I never felt that either of them was particularly interested in me for my own sake. I think my father wanted a son to whom he could talk baseball all the time. Both of my brothers satisfied that need for him. My mother's goal for me was that I become a nurse, since that was the career she had once wanted for herself. I rejected her aspirations for me and instead went to go to medical school and become a doctor. This was the advice I received from my grandmother, her mother. My grandmother once told me that she had been disappointed in both her daughters because "they had all the advantages" and could have gone into "any profession they wanted," but they gave it up for marriage. She said, "I worked hard to give them a better life than I had, and they never really appreciated that." My aunt had become a schoolteacher, and she once wrote a small book on the Missions of California, mostly for children; so I suspect that my grandmother was mostly disappointed in my mother's choices. Toward me, my grandmother was very loving and devoted; but not so toward either my mother or my aunt. I see that now in retrospect.

Grandma did not like either of the men her daughters had married, and she alternately feuded with them both, sometimes going years without speaking to one or the other of her daughters.

I think that Mary would have been there for all the women in my family, had any of them asked her to be. One psychological description that fits most of the people in my family—male and female—is a lack of personal insight that allows you to reflect on your own behavior. I have somewhat of a reputation within my family of being a "dreamer" with my head either in the clouds or in a book, but a lot of my thinking took me outside myself where I might be able to more accurately contemplate my own motives and desires. There is a reason I was known in the family as the "little professor" (besides the too-big glasses), and when I grew up, I actually became a professor.

Pauline settled down with one man for her entire life, and for most of it she lived as a devout Catholic. She and her husband Phil left the Church after the first big sexual scandal in the 80's and never returned. I remained close to them, however. I do not know the details of my Aunt Pauline's death, but I heard about it with great sadness. She was buried in the Catholic Church and in a Catholic cemetery eleven years after the death of my mother. Uncle Phil lived on for a number of years after that. When he was close to death, my cousins contacted my brother Paul and me, and we drove down to Riverside to see him one last time. The cousins had set up a hospital bed in his and Aunt Pauline's home in the front room, looking out over the rose bushes that my aunt had always loved. Uncle Phil was weak when we arrived, but as feisty and ornery as ever. I asked my cousin Margaret if they had called a priest for last rites. She told me that her father had absolutely refused to have a priest come. I was saddened by this and approached my uncle on my own to ask him if we could get a priest. He raised his voice and yelled at me, "No damn priest!" I patted him to signal ok, but in my heart, I thought that if he had been my father, I would have called a priest anyway. I sat next to him and silently prayed the Chaplet of Divine Mercy so that neither he nor my cousins could hear it. My brother and I stayed for a few hours then drove back home. We both knew that we would never see Uncle Phil again. He died two days later. I hope and pray that in those last moments before he died he made everything right with God. I pray for my father and mother and for my aunt and uncle all the time, and for my brothers and their families. Those in my family tree whom I don't know I have left to the intercession of the Immaculate Heart of Mary and the Mercy of God.

Had I become a surgeon instead of a psychiatrist, I probably would have forever focused on the "journey out" and external realities and banished all those uncomfortable internal realities that made me feel conflicted, but are so important in thinking about faith and God. That is why James the resident and Mary the patient (was her name a coincidence, I wonder? No, because when God is involved, there are no coincidences in life) were so important in my life. They caused me to think about more than the external realities of medicine and this world and accept that there is something more than pure naturalism. How can you measure love or caring? Yet these things are as real—maybe more so—as blood counts and x-rays.

I tried awfully hard to escape these internal naggings—the realities of my experience that constantly drew me towards a belief in God. How much further could I escape You, O Lord, than leaving the planet and venturing out into the vastness of Space? But even there You are lurking behind every planet and every star. Could I completely escape this world and not find You anyway? In Your great mercy, You sent Your Mother to bring me back to myself, to remind me of what it really means to be a woman and what is really important and matters in this life. She who knew all the pain and suffering a mother can possibly experience understood my pain and suffering and abandonment more than I could. She comforted me with roses and she re-parented me so that I could truly understand a mother's love, even though I had not been able to experience it in my own childhood. She helped me to forgive and let go of my resentments and anger toward those who were close to me and suffering in their own right, trying to cope with their own loveless lives. She did not pressure me, or insist that I turn away from any path I chose, but consistently placed other possibilities before me that would lead me off the track I was on and back onto the right path. "In my greatest sufferings, it seems to me that I no longer have a mother on this earth, but a very compassionate one in Heaven," Padre Pio reflected; and I feel the same way.

I feebly attempted to turn away from God, but, I was led back to the Cross anyway. How foolish I was to resist all those years, when a heavenly Father and Mother were there all the time. How insane to believe I was the master of my own fate when all my choices always seemed to lead me to unhappiness and regret. All I ever had to do was to look up and see Truth. And Lord, you kept me focused on Truth because whenever I would go my own way, Your precious Mother would always bring me back to the path You wanted me to take.

Mary, out of love for me and for all other lost and hopeless souls, you made yourself manifest in countless ways to comfort and encourage them and me as a loving mother would, to trust completely in your Son. "Do whatever he tells you."

And then on that unspeakably joyous day when the Father allowed me to hear His voice lovingly admonishing me, I knew I was on the right path toward home.

The End So Far

…And so I became a member of the Immaculata's Militia. One of the 144,000 took me up and introduced me to the real war and prepared me for battle with the true enemy. Mary is the 12-star General of these human troops. Our shield and weapons are the Word of God and the Rosary of Mary, the symbol of THE GARDEN and the dwelling place of God among us: the Church. Until He joins us in the Final Battle against the prince of this world, the evil that prowls around the world seeking the ruin of souls, I will fight proudly alongside Mary, my mother.

I have been welcomed back into the Catholic Church, a place of heaven on earth, where Christ in the Blessed Sacrament dwells. It is good that the Church is, among other things, a hospital for sinners. There was no banquet or feast then for my leap of faith, but I am conscious of my mother's constant love and continued encouragement. I hope to enjoy a sumptuous supper someday when the Father and Son greet me in the Kingdom. With a great deal of grace, even a sinner like myself can be forgiven and washed clean.

And perhaps one day, this prodigal daughter will be shown her special room in the mansion of heaven, where Christmas is celebrated eternally.

THE END (so far!)

APPENDIX

Bringing Mary Into Your Life

All who wish to bring Mary more deeply into their lives will find that there are many devotions and opportunities to do so in the Catholic Church. The advantages of having the Blessed Mother be a fundamental part of your life are so great, that it is amazing to me that there are those who reject her presence. Remember, Jesus spent 33 years on earth with His Mother, 30 more years than He spent in His ministry! As St. Maximilian Kolbe noted, "Never be afraid of loving Mary too much. You can never love her more than Jesus did."

Below are the devotions that I use, but I urge you to develop your own unique way of venerating Mary and using her intercession with the Father and the Son for you and your family, or for anyone.

1. **Pray the Rosary daily!**

   In her numerous apparitions, Our Lady repeatedly requests that the Rosary be prayed daily in order to convert sinners and to make atonement for sins. There are many resources available to help you pray, including smart phone apps and online sites. The incredible graces and benefits to yourself and the world of praying the Rosary daily are numerous. It changes lives (it changed mine) and is a powerful spiritual weapon against the evils of our time. Just do it!

2. **Marian Pilgrimages**

   a. Guadalupe

   b. Fatima

   c. Lourdes

   d. Other approved Marian sites

   Many Catholic organizations offer tours/pilgrimages to Marian sites around the world. If you have not seen the miraculous tilma of Our Lady of Guadalupe, then I recommend it for your first pilgrimage, as it is astonishing to behold.

3. Marian Consecration

33 Days to Morning Glory – Book by Fr. Michael Gaitley (preparation and consecration itself repeated annually)

Consecration is the act of making something holy. The process of Total Consecration to Mary was introduced by St. Louis de Montfort in the early part of the 18th century. De Montfort's classic work *True Devotion to Mary* is a formal act of consecration to Mary, so through her, one can be consecrated to Christ. There are a number of readily available books in addition to Gaitley's and de Montfort's, which take you through the process. I recommend *Marian.org* as a good website for obtaining resources.

4. The Brown Scapular

The word *scapular* is derived from the Latin word *scapula,* or shoulder blade. Monks used to wear two large pieces of cloth, attached at the shoulders by narrow strips, which covered the fronts and backs of their habits, to protect the habit from dirt and wear. However, this overgarment eventually became part of the habit itself. It is now common for those who want to associate themselves with a particular religious order or devotion to wear a miniature version of the scapular. It is considered a sacramental. There are now more than a dozen types of scapulars approved by the Church for a variety of devotions, but the original is the Brown Scapular of Our Lady of Mt. Carmel

According to tradition, a Carmelite priest, St. Simon Stock, was praying for his Order which was undergoing some trials and persecutions, when on July 16th, 1251, he received a visit from Our Lady. She handed him a Brown Scapular and said, "Receive, my beloved son, this Scapular of thy Order; it is the special sign of my favor, which I have obtained for thee and for thy children of Mount Carmel. *He who dies clothed with this habit shall be preserved from eternal fire.* It is the badge of salvation, a shield in time of danger, and a pledge of special peace and protection."

This apparition of the Blessed Virgin Mary is known as Our Lady of Mt. Carmel. This Marian devotion is quite widespread, even outside the Carmelite Order, due to the great promise given by Our Lady. Because of her promises to those who wear the Brown Scapular, the devotion spread to the laity as a sign of Marian devotion and consecration. To receive the benefits of the Scapular, the scapular must be blessed, and the one wearing it should be enrolled in the Confraternity of the Brown Scapular (see http://www.meditationsfromcarmel.com/content/scapular-catechesis).

5. **Daily Marian Prayers**

   a. *The Little Office of the Blessed Virgin Mary* is a liturgical devotion to the Blessed Virgin, in imitation of (and often prayed in addition to) the Divine Office in the Catholic Church. It is a recurring cycle of psalms, hymns, Scripture and other readings that are read daily throughout the day. Books on the Little Office can be obtained easily on Amazon and through most Catholic bookstores. It is not very time-consuming to follow the daily devotions, which not only reflect on Our Lady but also, always, conspicuously point to her Son.

   b. The *Angelus* prayer is said daily, three times a day, usually at 6 am, 12 noon and 6 pm. It is a way of letting Our Blessed Mother know we are thinking of her and honoring the moment in salvation history when her *fiat* brought the Incarnate Word into the world.

     ℣. *The Angel of the Lord declared unto Mary:*

     ℟. *And she conceived of the Holy Spirit.*

     Hail Mary, full of grace, the Lord is with thee. Blessed art thou among women and blessed is the fruit of thy womb, Jesus. Holy Mary, Mother of God, pray for us sinners now and at the hour of our death. Amen.

     ℣. *Behold the handmaid of the Lord.*

     ℟. *Be it done unto me according to thy word. Hail Mary....*

℣. *And the Word was made flesh,*

℟. *And dwelt among us. Hail Mary....*

℣. *Pray for us, O Holy Mother of God!*

℟. *That we be made worthy of the promises of Christ.*

Let us pray.

Pour forth we beseech Thee, O Lord, Thy grace into our hearts, that we, to whom the Incarnation of Christ Thy Son was made known by the message of an angel, may by His Passion and Cross be brought to the glory of His Resurrection, through the same Christ Our Lord. Amen.

6. Five First Saturdays Devotion:

Over one hundred years ago in 1917, Our Lady revealed herself to three young children at Fatima in a series of apparitions whose impact still resonates today. Her appearance occurred during one of the bloodiest and most horrific wars humankind had ever waged to that date. During one of the apparitions, she requested what are now known as the First Saturday Devotions, in order to make reparation for blasphemies and offenses against her Immaculate Heart and for world peace.

Why five? Our Blessed Mother told Lucia, one of the children, that the five Saturdays are to make reparation for the five kinds of offenses and blasphemies uttered against her Immaculate Heart. The offenses were later specified by Our Lord. They are:

1) blasphemies against her Immaculate Conception,

2) blasphemies against her perpetual virginity,

3) blasphemies against her Divine maternity,

4) blasphemies by those who openly seek to foster in the hearts of children indifference or even hatred for her, and

5) blasphemies by those who desecrate and dishonor her holy images.

This devotion was reinforced in 1926 when the Child Jesus appeared to Sister Lucia and emphasized the importance of making these reparations to His Mother's Immaculate Heart, in order that the world may have peace. Today, over one hundred years later, the blasphemies continue unabated and have become even more extreme and frequent: abortion, euthanasia, destruction of all aspects of the family, normalization of sexual perversions, and frequent satanic and atheistic attacks on our Holy Mother's person and image. Sometimes it seems as if everything is spiraling out of control, but the Blessed Virgin promised that reparation in the form of the First Saturday Devotion would bring about world peace and that she would personally *"at the hour of death [bring] the graces necessary for salvation"* to all those who fulfilled the devotion.

7. **Memorare:** this short prayer was traditionally written by St. Bernard and popularized in the 15th century. It reminds us that we have a powerful intercessor and protector in Mary. I say this prayer at the completion of every Rosary, when I ask for my special intentions.

> *Remember, O most gracious Virgin Mary,*
> *that never was it known*
> *that anyone who fled to thy protection,*
> *implored thy help, or sought thy intercession,*
> *was left unaided.*
> *Inspired with this confidence, I fly to thee,*
> *O Virgin of virgins, my Mother.*
> *To thee do I come, before thee I stand,*
> *sinful and sorrowful.*
> *O Mother of the Word Incarnate,*
> *despise not my petitions,*
> *but in thy mercy hear and answer me.*
> *Amen.*

8. **Books** – these are some of my favorite books about Mary (but there are many others!):

   a. *33 Days to Morning Glory* – Fr. Michael Gaitley

   b. *True Devotion to Mary* – St. Louis de Montfort

   c. *Hail Holy Queen* – Scott Hahn

   d. *Champions of the Rosary* – Fr. Donald Calloway

    e. *Mary: God's Yes to Man* (John Paul's encyclical, *Redemptoris Mater,* with an introduction by Joseph Cardinal Ratzinger)

    f. *The World's First Love: Mary, Mother of God* – Bishop Fulton J. Sheen